In My Small Corner

First published 2001 by
SCOTTISH CULTURAL PRESS
Unit 13d, Newbattle Abbey Business Annexe
Newbattle Road, DALKEITH EH22 3LJ Scotland
Tel: +44 (0)131 660 6366 • Fax: +44 (0)131 660 6414
Email: info@scottishbooks.com
website: www.scottishbooks.com

Copyright © Margaret Aitken, 2001
Margaret Aitken has asserted her right under the Copyright, Designs and Patents Act, 1988, to be identified as Author of this Work

All rights reserved. No part of this publication may be reproduced, stored in a retrieval system, or transmitted in any form or by any means, electronic, mechanical, photocopying, recording or otherwise, without the prior permission, in writing, of Scottish Cultural Press

BRITISH LIBRARY CATALOGUING IN PUBLICATION DATA
A catalogue record for this book is available from the British Library

ISBN: 1 84017 002 6

Printed and bound by Bell & Bain Ltd, Glasgow

IN MY SMALL CORNER

Memories of an Orkney Childhood

Margaret Aitken

SCOTTISH CULTURAL PRESS

Other Books by the Same Author

Six Buchan Villages
Twelve Light Years

Margaret Aitken's childhood was followed by three years at Moray House Teachers Training College, Edinburgh, after which she returned to Orkney.

Her marriage was the start of a very happy phase of her life about which she wrote in *Twelve Light Years* – an attempt to describe what it was like to be a lightkeeper's wife. During that time, some of her topographical, historical and biographical articles were published.

For the past thirty years Margaret and her husband have lived in Cruden Bay, Aberdeenshire. They both taught in Peterhead, and she wrote a history of their own and five neighbouring villages, entitled *Six Buchan Villages*. They have a son, Richard, and a daughter, Katherine.

Retirement has been busy and exciting. She has gained B.A. Honours (Open University), and has continued to write and publish articles. At present, she is having modest success with her children's stories, to the delight of her grandchildren, James and Sophie.

Acknowledgements

I wish to thank the following: the Editor of *The Orcadian*, Kirkwall, for permission to draw on articles by me first published in the pages of that newspaper; Mr Robert P. Rendall, nephew of the poet Robert Rendall, for permission to include two poems by Robert Rendall – 'Birsay' from *Country Sonnets and Other Poems* and 'The Planticru' from *Orkney Variants and Other Poems*.

This book is dedicated to my sister, Lilian, and to the memory of the other beloved members of the household at 'The Moorings' – my mother, father, aunt, grandparents, two great-uncles and my great-grandmother.

Prologue

Jesus bids us shine with a clear, pure light,
Like a little candle burning in the night.
In this world is darkness
So we must shine
You in your small corner
And I in mine.

When I was a child, more than seventy years ago, my 'small corner' was Orkney – that little archipelago usually shown in a box in the north-east corner of maps of Great Britain.

one

Steaming mounds of clapshot stuck about with succulent sausages were placed before each diner at the New Year's Tea. The long tables, white-clothed and bearing an abundance of sandwiches, scones, cakes and biscuits stretched in rows the length of the Salvation Army Hall. Willing helpers poured tea from large kettles, and after the Captain had asked the blessing we all tucked in with a will.

The Salvation Army Hall, spiritual home of my grandparents, was a warm, happy place on such occasions. It was there that as a child I found a fun side to life which, to a small extent, alleviated the deadly serious view of existence transmitted by the earnest sobriety of my parents' religious sect – the Brethren.

I always felt rather disappointed when my jolly, laughing Salvationist friends underwent a metamorphosis, and at their ordinary meetings preached at us vehemently and mercilessly till some poor sinners, overwhelmed by emotion or terror at their words, were led weeping to kneel at the Penitent Form or Mercy Seat – a wooden bench with 'JESUS SAVES' printed in large white letters on its back.

However, at the teas – Home League or New Year's – after the feast, which was accompanied by a joyful babble of conversation, the tables were cleared and we were all seated round the walls of the hall, leaving a large central bare area of uncovered wooden floor on which to play games. 'Take your partners for the Grand Old Duke of York,' the master of ceremonies would call, and we were off on an evening of laughter and music. We marched round, dropping a key in front of the next person we wanted to join the procession. We spun the platter and raced in fear and trembling to catch it while still spinning, and so avoid having to perform a forfeit. We romped joyously in opposite circles in 'The Jolly Miller' ready to grab a partner on the last word of the chorus:

And a-hunting we will go
A-hunting we will go
We'll catch a fox and put him in a box
And a-hunting we will go

before the jolly miller in the middle managed to seize you and made you spare man.

'Push the Business On', where you skipped round with a partner before passing forward to take a new one for the next march round, was disapproved of by some of our more sombre elders who decided it was too much like dancing.

The evening ended with a hymn – called a song by the Salvationists – and there followed a prayer and benediction usually pronounced by one of the officers.

I was so used to the terminology of the Salvation Army I never associated it with warfare. Quite unperturbed by its non-pacifist tones, I'd listen to my sweet-faced, lavender-and-lace grandmother who was Corps Secretary tot up her 'cartridges' – small, casual collections of money. *The War Cry* and *The Young Soldier* were regular reading. The Captain and Lieutenant we knew and usually respected, but a Major or someone of higher rank, coming to inspect the books and doings of the Corps, was someone held in awe. Corps Sergeant-Major, Colour Sergeant, Bandmaster, Corps Secretary, Corps Treasurer and Home

League Secretary were some of the promoted posts to which senior and junior soldiers could aspire.

I don't wonder that the Salvation Army, with its ranks, military terms, marching, and waving flag, appealed to my grandfather. He had chosen to be a soldier in the service of Her Majesty Queen Victoria – 'The good owld queen' – whom he revered. Before he'd met my beautiful, young grandmother, he'd served in India. My grandmother and a girlfriend had, 'for a laugh' as she put it, gone to hear their fortunes from an old German woman called Babby Plank who lived in Kirkwall. Babby, among other things, told my grandmother that a tall, fair-haired man was coming from a far-off, hot country and she would marry him. Sure enough, my tall, strapping, fair-haired grandfather returned to Orkney from India and met my grandmother. They fell in love for life and soon were married.

He became a stone mason – fishing or turning his very capable hands to anything he could to tide them over the months of inclement weather when it was impossible to follow the building trade.

However, still a reservist when the Boer War broke out, he was again called to the colours and, leaving his young wife and baby daughter, sailed for South Africa. He kept a journal which he introduced as: '2nd Brigade Seaforth Highlanders, South Africa. The following is an account of our travels and doings during the South African Campaign 1899:1900:1901.' In it, a piece of history comes to life. The faded writing in the old jotter not only records events, but also the thoughts and feelings of a young soldier at the turn of the century, and reveals the climate of thought at that time as expressed by those in authority around him.

Here and there he has written out the speeches of high-ranking and titled people who addressed the soldiers, and I rather think their sentiments were accepted by him as being the right way to think. On 13 December, 1899, Lord Methuen, having inspected the brigade, sympathised with the men on the loss of their general – General Wauchope – when, on 11 December, a regiment of about a thousand, consisting of Black Watch, Seaforth Highlanders, Highland Light Infantry and Argyll and Sutherland Highlanders set out from the Modder River to engage with the Boers. The enemy opened fire at 200 yards, and the Scottish soldiers lay under fire for eleven hours without food or water. When eventually they retired to a place of safety, roll was called, and it was found that about 260 were either killed or missing.

Lord Methuen admitted in his speech that a blunder had been committed but completely exonerated the dead general. He concluded: 'There are three things you have to think of before yourselves and these are – your Queen, your country and the honour of your regiments. You may die and I may die but the honour of your regiments will live forever. If someone had given the word "advance" instead of "retire", it would have been a short and sure victory for British arms. However, that position must be taken at any cost and I can only say as Henry VIII said to his men long ago, 'Let every one do his best.'''

Conan Doyle's classic *The Great Boer War* confirms my grandfather's account of the tragic debacle. On 10 December, as they set out, 'rain fell heavily' through the whole dreadful night. Conan Doyle conveys a miserable picture: 'It was raining hard, and the men with one blanket between two soldiers bivouacked upon the cold damp ground, about three miles from the enemy's position. At one o'clock, without food, and drenched, they moved forwards through the drizzle and the darkness to attack those terrible lines.

'Clouds drifted low in the heavens, and the falling rain made the darkness more impenetrable.'

Little wonder that my grandfather suffered agonies with rheumatism in his latter years. Little wonder that, to the consternation of all the family, he insisted on standing fearlessly outside to watch the German Junkers strafe the beach below our house with machine-gun bullets, or that he remarked wryly of the Second World War troops: 'They're not proper soldiers. They're carted everywhere in trucks.'

'Feb. 4th 1900. Leave camp at 5 a.m., march a distance of about 20 miles, camp for night at Koodesberg drift.

'Feb. 14th. Reveille 3.13 a.m., marched to the Riet River a distance of about 14 miles.

'Feb. 15th. Resumed march the same night arriving in camp at 4.30 a.m. (Orange Drift).

'Feb. 17th. Received orders to march to Jacobsdale. We left at 2.30 a.m. a distance of 5 miles. Latterly order cancelled we marched 18 miles, camped beside river 7 miles from Kimberley.

'Oct 4th. We march at 2 p.m. – 10 miles.
'Oct. 5th. 6 a.m. march 12 miles.
'Oct. 6th. March 10 miles.
'Oct. 7th. 3 a.m. march 18 miles.
'Oct 8th. 8 a.m. march 12 miles.'

It would seem that my grandfather held no resentment over the long, gruelling marches or the miserable travel in wagons with about 20 men in each – 'there is not the least comfort' – and lying on the side of kopjes without blankets while heavy rain poured down.

They took towns – some of the men barefoot – and all starving; from 5 to 15 June 1900, they lived on one biscuit per man and a couple of ounces of Kaffir meal per day. On the 16th, my grandfather records, 'Black Watch arrive with convoy. Not before time. We almost felt like going out to graze with the animals.'

On 2 April 1901 he surprisingly makes his only reference to Pretoria. 'Leave Ellandsfontein arriving at Pretoria 1 p.m. Wed. 3, 4, 5 and 6 In Barracks.' I say surprisingly for I've heard my mother say he was at the taking of Pretoria, and he called her, his second daughter, Daisy Pretoria Groat.

On 16 May 1901 he wrote jubilantly: 'Expect to leave tomorrow for Capetown. En Route for home. Hallelujah.' On 31 December he writes:

'I know not what of trial or joy
May lie before me in the untrod way
But this I know
Sufficient grace is mine for each
succeeding day
So on His love I lay me down and say
God will be with me through the coming year
Lead me Oh Lord in thine own perfect way
With thee I have no fear.'

The initials 'A. J.' appear at the end of this verse, but I don't know who composed the piece. However, it expressed my grandfather's rock-hard faith. That stout faith no doubt supported him through all the hardships of the war, when 'their bullets fell amongst our feet like hail'; when 'the Boers crept down a nullah and hid themselves in the adjacent houses and about daybreak they opened doors and windows and fired on our men lying asleep on the ground'; and even when the soldier side of him was uppermost, and he felt let down, as on 14 September 1900: 'Leave for Brandfort arriving about 9 p.m., march out about twelve miles near Karee siding, lay by railway all night expecting enemy to cross but were doomed to disappointment they did not come our way.'

He sent home a beautiful card containing 'Silver Leaves from Table Mountain' and much later, about forty years after his return, in fact, this same card lay in my young hands. I remarked to him how many wonderful and extraordinary sights he must have seen. He replied, 'Oh the hills might be a bit higher and the rivers wider, but the only true satisfaction in life is to know your soul is saved.'

So it was not surprising that when he returned to civilian life he chose to continue marching, this time under the Salvation Army's banner of 'Blood and Fire', and played his silver cornet in praise of his God and in challenge against the powers of evil.

He told me of his religious conviction while he sat in his Victorian chair by the fireside, while above his head hung a picture depicting the Union Jack, the flag of the Duke of Albany's Regiment (which included the Seaforth Highlanders) and the badge of the Seaforths. This picture had been presented to the 1st Battalion Seaforth Highlanders by Her Majesty the Queen at Osborne on 16 August, 1884.

It was only in his later years when, crippled with rheumatism, that my grandfather sat idly in his chair. Most of his leisure time he'd spent out in his paraffin lamp-lit shed making beautiful and successful model racing-yachts. In our family we have several of the silver and gold medallions which he won and had made into brooches and pendants for us. He also built a full-scale racing yacht, and took part in local regattas winning trophy cups on occasion with the graceful 'Pretoria'.

It was his love of sailing and the sea that led him to design and build our house by the side of Kirkwall Bay – a house appropriately called 'The Moorings'. Here he could enjoy the most perfect view of the yachts sailing in the bay.

But his clever hands often worked for his grandchildren. I'll never forget the Christmas morning I came down to a beautiful doll's bed with two little chairs beside it on which I could sit. The doll in the bed had been dressed by my grandmother who had also sewn the bed linen, blankets and quilt.

If anything broke, weeping was usually stopped with the words 'Dedy'll know what to do – he'll mend it'. Hardly ever was he stumped, even constructing cloth heads to replace smashed china ones of beloved dolls. He could knit and mend socks; he could embroider; he made colourful rag rugs; and each summer he cycled miles to the Orphir moors, where he cut and prepared enough peats to keep our fire blazing all winter.

My grandfather was a heroic figure to me – a tower of strength on which I leaned. He spoke very rarely, but when he did we all listened.

two

A favourite seat of my grandfather's was at his bedroom window at the front of 'The Moorings'. There at night he trained his telescope on the moon and stars, and during the day kept a watch on the shipping in Kirkwall Bay.

I don't suppose he was as fascinated as I by the sad, wooden ribs of sunken ships that stuck out of the water. My mother had told me the tragic story of how, when she was a young girl, the *Kathleen Annie*, laden with spirits, caught fire and the *Busy Bee,* bravely going to her assistance, had also ignited and perished.

In contrast, very alive and prosperous looked the massive German and French liners – gigantic vessels with enormous superstructures and many funnels that hove to in the mouth of the bay on fine summer days. Packed launches brought the tourists to the pier, and the streets were suddenly pungent with foreign tobaccos.

In one dark, little shop, presided over by a friend of mine, Mary Foulis – a small, frail, bent, elderly woman with a long, pale face and wispy grey hair – I watched fascinated as two German ladies tried agitatedly to buy two 'steeks' emphasising the 'two' by pushing a couple of fingers under Mary's bewildered nose. At long last the purchase became clear. They wanted to buy a pair of brass candlesticks displayed in the crowded window.

Mary showed the same amused patience with me when it came to my Christmas shopping. Each year, with no demur, she led me across the shop so that my mother, left at the opposite counter a few feet distant, would not be apprised of the surprise in store for her on Christmas morning. Saving at the rate of tuppence a week for the purpose, Christmas shopping presented Mary and me with many problems. One year, a lidded jam dish encircled with superimposed china forget-me-nots, the knob on its lid consisting of one blue flower – a thing of great beauty in my estimation – had to be procured for my mother. Somehow Mary made it a possible purchase, but oh the agony of soul on the way home to realise that nothing had been bought for my dearly loved father, and sixpence was all that remained in my purse. A packet of 'Capstan' was the only answer – a completely guilt-free gift in those days for we didn't know the health risk associated with tobacco. Every year at the festive season various business acquaintances presented my grateful father with beautifully made wooden boxes divided into little sections all filled with neatly arranged rows of slim, white cigarettes or sometimes plump, golden-brown cigars.

He was aware that the Brethren disapproved of his smoking, but he scorned to hide his failing from them, and smoked quite openly. With a resigned sigh, as he lit another cigarette, he would say, 'Many's the time in the trenches we'd rather have a fag than our dinner.' He'd then go on to describe the frightful food served up to the soldiers during the 1914–18 holocaust.

Despite such memories, he remained proud throughout his life of having been a Royal Scot. He'd lied about his age in order to become one, and spent his nineteenth birthday in the trenches in France. 'We were known as Pontius Pilate's bodyguard,' he'd tell us proudly. 'The first of foot, the right of the line and the pride of the British army.' He had a simple response to the plea of any pacifist: 'What man would stand back and let anybody harm his wife and bairns? Call that a man!'

He was a small man – not above 5 foot 6 inches – but every inch he bore as a trained soldier, always holding himself ram-rod straight and marching along swiftly and smartly, his hair kept neatly trimmed and his clothes immaculate. He never forgot his training as a machine gunner, and though completely devoid of competence with mechanical things, years later could rattle off the instructions for taking apart and reassembling a Lewis gun.

His courage was never in doubt, and he faced bravely both life and death, which, as it approached, made him so weak he could scarcely walk. Vexed by such weakness he said sadly, 'I never thought I'd become a wash-out like this,' but he never failed to maintain the erect bearing of a soldier as he faded away.

My mother told me that during the First World War the American fleet lay some time in Kirkwall Bay. Then, when the Second World War came, I remember how the normal boat population of southward-bound ships (known as the 'sooth boats') and those plying to and fro to the islands – the 'north isle boats' – was again greatly increased. Bustling little drifters made mysterious exits and entrances. Though we once had a crew member staying with us I don't think any of us ever knew the business of those ex-fishing boats which tied up each night at Kirkwall pier.

Grey warships also appeared at the entrance to the bay, and when darkness fell, awesomely segmented the night sky with powerful paths of light beamed out by their great searchlights.

In past times, ships did not stop when they came to Kirkwall Bay, but sailed on into what is known as the 'Peedie Sea'. In March 1722, however, the 'Magistrats and Counsell' ordered Kirkwallians to take their spades and shovels and clear 'the oyce mouth'. The entrance to the Peedie Sea harbour was so silted up with gravel, sand and stones that 'ships and great boats' could scarcely manage to get in or out even 'at a full sea'. During 1807–1809 subscriptions were requested for the building of a pier in Kirkwall, and in 1813 and 1814 a second pier, the West Pier, was built to shelter shipping in the harbour from westerly gales.

A great day was planned to celebrate the starting of the first pier, which George Burns, the architect, had offered to construct for three thousand, four hundred and fifty pounds sterling. The masonic brethren of Kirkwall Kilwinning Lodge were to walk in procession to the ceremony of laying the pier's foundation stone, and later were to join the Magistrates and Council for dinner along with the officers of the military presence at that time in the town. Soldiers were to line the streets through which the procession would pass.

However, up to 1867, Kirkwall's pier was not all that satisfactory. At that date, the *St Magnus* – a paddle steamer with two funnels – was the first of the North of Scotland and Orkney and Shetland Steam Navigation Company's steamers to come alongside a new pier which unlike its predecessor, was not dependent on the tides. Up till then Kirkwall had been an 'anchor' port where the cargoes and passengers of steamers had to be brought ashore in small boats.

The clanking, rattling sounds of winches and other machinery as ships loaded and unloaded at Kirkwall pier was the background noise against which we daily lived in our house out Cromwell's Road.

Yes, fellow Kirkwallians, Cromwell's Road! My persistence in using our road's correct appellation cost me a precious mark in a composition in Class 6. On the sign it said 'Cromwell's Road', and as that gentleman had built a fort and positioned a garrison in the vicinity, I thought it appropriate that the road should be said to be his, as it very likely was named after him when his troops were stationed by it. The teacher of Class 6, like the majority of Kirkwall people, called it 'Cromwell Road'. I always regret that I didn't have the courage to say to a local painter about to refurbish the sign as I passed by – 'Don't miss out the "s".' I felt sure he would because of the common usage and, sure enough, he did. And so it's been unimaginatively 'Cromwell Road' ever since – a pity for it's a road that can stir the imagination just a little bit. No doubt Cromwell's Roundheads marched along it, and galloped over it on the horses they stabled in the cathedral.

On 11 February 1725, a great gun kept at the Mount – the promontory that juts out from the road on the east side of the bay – was hauled along it to be positioned at a fort by the shore in readiness for the undesired arrival of the pirate John Gow.

Service men of both world wars trod it, and the Territorial Army camp was positioned by it. Huge, circular, concrete tables on which we jumped and played at the Mount (pronounced 'Munt') had been emplacements for World War I territorial guns. A little further along the road once stood the Kirkwall Coast Guard Station.

German bombers mistook Cromwell's Road for the aerodrome at the opposite side of the bay, and dropped bombs in the fields round the house of 'Craigiefield' (usually referred to by my parents as 'Hossacks' for it had been built by and had been the home of Mr B. H. Hossack, writer of that splendid history, *Kirkwall in the Orkneys*). Further on, nearer where Cromwell's road wound to its end, a daffodil-bordered avenue led from white gateposts to the hospitable farmhouse of 'Greenfield', a generous, warm abode where, during the war, many service men were made welcome and luxuriated in home comforts.

Nearer the town than my home, there lived in 'Cromwell Cottage' another historian, Mr John Mooney, author of *St Magnus Earl of Orkney* and other titles. Not bad – two notable historians from one road!

In another house lived a girl called Kathleen Silver whose surname seemed so fitting when one heard her beautiful, silvery voice singing. Kathleen, Elsie, Nan and Helen were the 'big girls' out our road. What joy when we small fry were allowed to enter Elsie's shed to play shops with little jars and bottles of seeds of grasses or stand in a circle for ball games. Once, very early on, they must have regretted their tolerance of me. They took me to the Bay of Meal – a sandy beach about a mile or so from our homes. The fun had hardly begun when I cut a toe on a sharp stone. As the blood flowed alarmingly I howled, and there was nothing for it but pack up and hasten home with their bawling charge.

Attractive, stoutly built houses lined one side of Cromwell's Road. A black, wooden fence separated its other edge from the grassy, flower-spattered banks that sloped down to the stony beach beneath. Tangy smells wafted on the sea breezes that cooled it on summer days. Salt spray whipped across our faces when the bay heaved and surged grey-green and white-frothed to the wintry shore and threatened the crumbling, clay cliffs, the bastions on which the road and its sturdy, gardened villas depended.

All such anxieties forgotten, their gleaming windows reflected the sun as it set in the late, late twilight of the northern summer. Cromwell's Road to the point of Carness on one side, purple Wideford Hill, Hatston, the point of Crowness and the deep blue hills of Rendall and of the island of Rousay on the other, embraced the sheltered bay now awash with golds, crimsons, pale lemons and faded rose pinks emanating from the sinking sun and glowing sky.

I knew and loved 'wir road' well. I was acquainted with every quirk in its paving stones. So it came as a shock when, after an absence of some years, I overheard a resident's little girl enquire as I passed by – 'Who's that lady?'

three

Seeing ships glide prettily into Kirkwall Bay didn't fool me one bit about sea travel. My very limited experience had taught me that those same smooth sailing vessels could heave and roll, and their journey would end by carrying me to the pier – a miserable hump of humanity, so sea-sick I just wished everything would come to an end. The thought of the dreaded return journey always intruded into my otherwise happy holidays.

The earliest outing by ship that I remember was a day trip to the island of Eday. This event remains fresh in my mind for two reasons. The first, which made me feel quite fearful, was that the family we were visiting had had the horrifying experience of lightning coming down their chimney and killing the dog by the fireside. The other reason was a pleasant one. The boy and his sister, whose names I can't recall, took me out to the barn where I discovered a litter of kittens. I was allowed to choose one – 'Poma' – a grey and white ball of fur which I took home and loved dearly and sincerely for many years.

The next sea journey on which I was very sick-sick was to the island of Westray. In an exhibition of art work in our school I once saw a poster which called Westray 'Queen of the Islands'. To me, that sounded just right, for, with its creamy stretches of sand and beaches built up with rack upon rack of sea-scoured, sea-smoothed, clean, clean boulders, Westray was a beautiful island.

When I was four, my parents and I holidayed in the pure white Pierowall Hotel in the village of the same name. Next to the hotel was a shop owned by a silver-haired gentleman called Mr Robertson. His shop, too, was pure, clean white. My father always walked with a silver-topped walking stick, and I, all admiration, longed to be able to emulate his movements – now daintily tapping the road, now flicking smartly upwards, sometimes swinging a bit or, on occasion, twirling. I expressed my terrible longing for a walking stick so insistently that we ended by visiting Mr Robertson. Here, I seem to remember, was a circular rail hung about with the desired objects. At last one was chosen – much too long for a four year old, but that didn't matter, for Mr Robertson assured me he'd soon have it tailored to fit. My pride in that stick knew no bounds.

Unfortunately, not even my stick could help me to muster enough strength to walk the seemingly endless miles from Noup Head Lighthouse, which we visited, back to the village. To climb the lighthouse itself had been an endurance test. Hard, bare stone steps spiralled up and up, higher and higher, higher and higher, until dizziness overcame me. The kindly lightkeeper came to my rescue, picking me up and carrying me to the top. I was dazzled by gleaming glass and by highly polished, bright and shining copper jugs and brass trays that stood about or hung from white, white walls.

The long homeward journey was the price waiting to be paid for such beauty, but I had only gone a short distance when, almost crying with weariness, I collapsed by the side of the road, refusing to take one more step. All these years later, I remember my overwhelming relief when a large, blue, red-wheeled cart trundled toward us. My father asked the driver if he'd give me a lift, and in a trice I was hoisted up among a large brood of carrot-haired children.

It seemed to me that people in Westray at that time surely had large families. I remember on one visit looking up from my low 'creepie' in a farmhouse kitchen to a long row of swinging, black-stockinged legs. When we came to leave that large household the father brought out his pony and gig to carry us back to the village. As we clip-clopped through the gathering dusk, a candle flickering on each side of the vehicle, I wouldn't, as the saying goes, 'have called the King my cousin'. Thereafter, every evening in our hotel room I happily drove a 'gig' constructed of our suitcases and a length of string.

Our bedroom opened off the dining-room in which there was one enormous table at which all guests dined. So everybody had to get to know everybody else to some extent. Mr Stanley Cursiter, the Orcadian artist who became Queen's Limner of Scotland, and his wife were fellow diners. I recall being taken to his room one day to wish him 'good morning' as he was unable to come to the dining-room, being in the grips of a bout of lumbago.. A small incident, perhaps, but one which stands out in my mind nearly seventy years on for his kindness in taking notice of a shy child like me.

I also met Mr Allen, a commercial traveller in 'real' life who turned out to be an expert at building sand-castles. I remember feeling rather discouraged on realising that my efforts in that field would never come up to his castellated, moat-surrounded edifices. However, he made me laugh a great deal, and I was fond of him.

The girl who waited at table was the proprietor's sweet-natured daughter, Olive. So taken was I with this young lady I thought Olive was surely the prettiest name a girl could have. Olive used to bring me a glass of hot milk and some Abernethy biscuits before I went to bed. How I enjoyed that!

There were soft, summer mornings when my parents sat on a grassy bank by a rutted track, and conversed uninterrupted to their heart's content, for nearby, I'd found a great mass of the most delightful, fluffy, feathery yellow flowers. It was years and years later that I discovered they were Lady's Bedstraw, the sight of which still brings back the feelings of delight I'd felt on discovering them in Westray.

Some days we went to a flat stretch of smooth, fawn sands. A little house stood nearby out of which tumbled a host of children who formed a fairly sizeable ring into which my father gently but firmly pushed me. We'd pass a ball round and across our circle, my father keeping a watchful eye lest anybody decided to do anything more jolly or daring and so terrify his timid offspring.

I doubt if anything the children could have done would have scared me as much as the boat trip he took us on to the small nearby island of Pharay. We climbed into a rowing boat, and the father of the family with the gig plied the oars. I'd never been before in a small open boat, and it wasn't long till the choppy waves seemed to me to have reached dangerous proportions. 'Please ask Jesus to say, "Peace be still",' I begged. Nobody would, even though to my eyes they all seemed rather ill at ease.

We did, eventually, arrive on the island where the entire population had crowded into the small, one-roomed school to hear my father preach. My impression was of a mass of dark serge suits in the midst of which my father spoke earnestly, rivulets of sweat running down his face, for the day was hot as well as the room being packed with people.

My parents' usual religious home in Westray was the meeting house of the Brethren which I think was on the outskirts of the village of Pierowall. There I liked to see my friend Murdoch with his scrubbed, pink, moustachioed face which didn't seem to me to look as right above a starched collar and dark Sabbath suit as it did when we were greeted by him in his every day, collarless, grey, flannelette shirt.

Murdoch's whitewashed cottage was at the edge of the village. We had to cross a small bridge to reach it. Inside was cool and shadowy – the walls a distempered pale green, the little windows white-lace curtained. Glasses of frothing milk and boiled eggs were the fare at Murdoch's on bee-buzzing, hen-fluttering summer afternoons.

I remember a hill – Fitty Hill – on which my father challenged me to beat him to the summit, and then made quite sure that I arrived there before him. There was a great, gloomy castle – Noltland Castle

– dark and foreboding, its walls impregnated with past wickedness. I shuddered in its dark, dank depths, though I then knew nothing of the atrocities of the sixteenth century when it was built by Gilbert Balfour, brother-in-law to Bishop Bothwell and one time 'Maister Household' to Queen Mary. But Noltland Castle's dark shadow was the only one cast on the beautiful island of Westray of my childhood.

As I look back, I only remember journeys on both the *Earl Thorfinn* and *Earl Sigurd* as taking place on dark-blue seas beneath clear, sunny skies. Rose-coloured as those memories are, I wonder which Earl Thorfinn or Earl Sigurd those ships commemorated in real life. We have a choice.

There was the first Norse Earl of Orkney, Sigurd the Mighty whose demise was perhaps the most remarkable thing about him. He was riding back from a battle with the head of his enemy slung from his saddle. His victim, Maelbrigte Tusk, had been buck-toothed and one of his protruding teeth pierced Sigurd's leg. Inflammation set in, and he died as a result of his wound. He was buried in a mound on the banks of the River Oykel on the borders of Sutherland and Caithness.

There was a later Sigurd – Sigurd the Stout – who had a nasty surprise when King Olaf of Norway invited him aboard his galley in the vicinity of Scapa Flow. Olaf seized the Earl's son, and stated that either Sigurd become a Christian immediately or he'd kill his son. Sigurd had no option. He became a Christian with great alacrity, and allowed himself to be baptised. However, it was under the pagan raven banner, woven to the accompaniment of magic spells by his mother, that he perished in Ireland. As Audna had said when she gave the banner to him, they who followed it would always be victorious, but they who bore it were doomed to die. As standard bearer after standard bearer fell, Sigurd finding that no one would obey his order to bear the banner, carried it himself, and was very quickly pierced through with a spear.

The earliest Earl Thorfinn was known as Thorfinn Skullsplitter. Perhaps surprisingly, with a name like that, he died on a sick bed. However, he goes down in history as a great and warlike chief highly regarded by his subjects.

The other Earl Thorfinn started early his career as a ruler. When five years old, his grandfather, Malcolm II of Scotland, gave him the Earldom of Caithness. It wasn't long till he was laying claim to part of the Earldom of Orkney, and after a period of years overcame the opposition and took over the entire earldom.

Repentant of the deeds which he'd perpetrated to achieve his ambitions, he made a pilgrimage to Rome to receive absolution from the Pope, and on his return turned his attentions to administering his domains, considering the needs of his subjects, and building Christ's Kirk in Birsay. He died in 1064 – an earl of 'seventy winters' and considered by the saga writer as the most powerful earl and the one whose lands extended further than those of any other.

I gave no thought to those famous Norsemen as I, now in my teens, sailed away for a second visit to the island of Eday. Unlike the previous trip, this one took place in dense fog.

As the ship nosed its way slowly northwards some service men entertained my two girlfriends and me. One remark we found hilariously funny was when a young army lieutenant wished he had brought – and he mimed playing an accordion – 'my go-fae-me come-tae-me'.

We arrived at the island, and made our way from the pier along deep pink sandstone roads to the croft home of one of my companions. Here we were welcomed warmly by grannie, father, mother, two sisters and a brother. They were kind, homely folk and the atmosphere in that house was one of warmth and contentment.

The mist cleared through the day, but closed in again when evening came. We all said goodnight and retired at a reasonable hour. One of my friends and I shared a bed. We had just nestled under the covers when she astounded me by asking – 'You'll no' be frightened if the boys come?'

The boys – what boys – and why were they coming?

She giggled, and then explained that in country places boys often visited girls at night. She and some friends had experienced such a visit once before in another rural district.

'What did they do?' I asked in amazement.

'They tickled our feet,' was the reply.

She'd hardly finished speaking when the room was lit up by powerful torches. Dark figures loomed through the mist and crowded round the small window. I was frightened. The top half of the window was lowered, and one of the visitors started trying to move pots of geraniums that stood on the window sill. The torches went out. I sprang from the bed, and, promptly floodlit, ran through to the kitchen where her parents slept.

'There are boys trying to come in through our window,' I panted shakily, whereupon the son of the house made for the door and rattled the bolt as though about to go out. The window was clear when I returned to our bedroom, but not before my bedfellow in my absence had doused the first intruder with a jug of cold water. She was not going to encourage a repeat of her first tickling experience, whatever the youths of Eday had in mind!

In contrast, the following Sunday morning was sunny, calm and peaceful. Grannie was a Baptist. Father, mother and two sisters were Brethren, as were my two companions and myself (the young man of the house had not, as yet, actually joined the Brethren, although he did attend their meetings). Hatted and dressed in our Sabbath clothes, we all, except grannie, made our way along a trodden path across fields to a stone cottage. Inside, a peat fire blazed, and in front of it stood a white-clothed table bearing a large glass of red wine and a plate on which was a chunk of white bread. Wooden forms were arranged on either side of the table and in rows in the centre of the room.

Simply and sincerely those good island people worshipped and partook of the sacrament. Brethren Assemblies do not have a minister, vicar, pastor or clergyman by any name to lead their worship. They sit in silence or with eyes closed in silent prayer until, as they believe, the Holy Spirit moves them to announce a hymn from their 'Believers' Hymn Book' to be sung unaccompanied by any musical instrument, or say a prayer or read from the Bible. Then about half-way through their 'morning meeting' some male will ask God's blessing on the bread, will go to the table, break the bread with his hands into two parts and give a half to the nearest person on each of the benches on either side of the table. Each worshipper then pinches a small piece out of the bread with his fingers, eats it and passes on the bread to the next person. Then the same man who first broke the bread gives thanks for 'the cup' and the glass of wine makes its round of the congregation, each member taking a sip before passing the glass on to his or her neighbour.

The Apostle Paul – a considerable influence on the conduct of Brethren Assemblies – states somewhere something to the effect 'Let not a woman's voice be heard in the church'. So too bad if you happen to be female with something you badly want to say. You are not allowed to open your mouth in a Brethren meeting – not even when it's one ironically called 'A Discussion Circle'.

As our Eday holiday progressed, we were taken visiting and enjoyed the generous and warm hospitality of the people of Eday. We visited a house retained as it had been through many generations. The kitchen floor was made of black flag-stones sprinkled over with silver sand. The fireplace was a large, open one with a kettle hanging on a hook over the blazing peats in the centre of the hearth. The entire fireplace was pure white except for one smoke-blackened central line stretching from the fire up and into the chimney.

Another small cottage close by the sea seemed very small indeed when its tall occupants – mother, father and three stalwart daughters – were all inside. The father was a fisherman and his second daughter accompanied him to sea; the results of their work could be seen hanging in rows from the rafters, drying.

One summer's evening we sang as we marched and skipped along the quiet pink roads arm in arm after visiting an elderly couple and their only son. The young man 'following us home', as accompanying departing guests for part of their homeward journey was called in Orkney, remarked rather sadly, 'We'll mak' up for this fun on the long, winter nights.' This attitude seemed overly morose to me until I remembered the limited social life on the island. The house neighbouring that of my friend's was also inhabited by an elderly couple and their only child – a daughter. Hers was no life of luxury; many a day we saw Daisy out ploughing with her pair of oxen – 'the nowt' as they were called in Eday.

One of our visits was to Carrick Farm near Carrick House – a place which played a central role in one of Eday's more exciting incidents, as I was to discover much later.

In February 1725 Mr James Fea, who lived in Carrick House, had some anxious days after John Gow, an old schoolfellow, threatened to pay him a visit. 'Threatened' because John Gow was a pirate who had assured his crew of ruffians that if they came to these northern waters he'd direct them to unguarded houses near the shore and well worth plundering. It would seem that Carrick House fell into this category.

However, Pirate Gow made a nautical blunder and grounded his ship, *The Revenge*, in a strait between the island of Eday and a small islet called the Calf of Eday. Soon a message arrived from the stranded ship requesting a boat to tow her out of the channel of Calf Sound. Mr Fea sent back the first of many letters he was to write to John Gow in the next three days; he concluded this missive, 'you shall not want my assistance, so far as honour can allow me. No more, but that I am your old school comrade.'

On the contrary, honour would not permit James Fea to help his old school mate in the slightest. Already a plan was hatching in the mind of the master of Carrick House.

On sighting a boat from the pirate ship approaching, he had his own vessel scuttled, and the oars from all other small boats removed and hidden. He adopted a friendly attitude towards the well-armed brigands which enabled him to entice them to a nearby public house, and there ply them with ale. He maintained his placatory tone in the epistles he continued to send Captain Gow, who, pleading for boats to help him refloat *The Revenge* or at least make it possible for him to escape, offered Fea a thousand pounds and twenty pence per day to every man who came to his aid.

James Fea persisted with his soft, cunning words until he succeeded in persuading Pirate Gow to come ashore himself where, of course, he was immediately overcome and made prisoner. James Fea then forced his captive to write to the men still on the pirate vessel telling them that he could not get a boat till they all came on to the island of Eday. This lie brought the desired result, and the episode drew to a close with all the pirates captured.

The bell of *The Revenge* remained in Carrick House for many years afterwards, and one of James Fea's helpers became possessor of John Gow's telescope. The pirate captain's sea-chest is preserved in Stromness museum. When I was a small child, my father used to lift me up so I could see through a window in the wholesale department of the business in which he worked. Down below us was a garden, but it was the object in the centre which drew my eye. There stood a little building of grey stone decorated with white sea-shells. This edifice's tall, cone-shaped roof had been built of the ballast taken from John Gow's ship.

four

Not all my reluctant sea-journeys were as uneventful as those I've told you about. On Saturday morning, 4 July, 1936, my parents, my young sister and I – eight years old at the time – going 'sooth' to Edinburgh for our summer holidays, started our journey on the *St Ola*.

Since my grandmother advised that 'It's aalways far cowlder on the sea,' my sister and I were accordingly cocooned in coats, scarves, 'tammies' and so on as though it were the depths of winter. We caught P. F. Thomson's bus for the *Ola*, and were transported to Scapa pier. There lay the SS *St Ola*, belching black smoke from her funnel, her black belly reposing on a grey, oil-silk sea, while the rest of her nestled in damp wads of chill sea-mist.

'Do we have to go out in that?' I asked anxiously, indicating the all enveloping fog.

'There's nothing to worry about,' replied my father. 'Why, Captain Swanson knows the Firth like the back of his hand.'

'I don't want to go.'

'It'll be all right,' my mother countered soothingly.

We boarded the *Ola*, took seats on deck near the stern and soon were on our way, cutting sightlessly out into Scapa Flow. I huddled by my parents on a hard bench along the rails on the port side. Attempts were made to persuade me that going on holiday was a good idea, something to be enjoyed, but I resisted all and was quite relieved to be left to my own miserable meditations.

Outwith that small, fog-enclosed world of the ship, all that was to be seen was grey-green water undulating away from the base of the boat. Inside was similarly bleak; brasses gleamed weakly, salty dew-beads hung from ropes and railings, and passengers formed small groupings.

There were only two of my fellow passengers in whom I took any interest. One was Mr John Spence of St Margaret's Hope, one of whose hands shook continuously, but whom I liked. The other was a long, lanky, dark-haired young man who sprawled in one deckchair while another supported his injured leg encased in plaster.

The only sounds were the murmur of voices, the swishing of the disturbed sea and the throbbing of the ship's engines. Then, all at once, came a cry from the bow – 'Land Ahead!'

A moment later, the ship reared up in front and gave great sideways lurches. My mother, with my sister on her knee, slid round the stern, my father disappeared through a cabin doorway, and I found myself hanging on to the rails in terror.

The captain, looking very worried, came down from the bridge, and gave the order to 'lower the lifeboats'. Seamen appeared from the innards of the vessel and started to unfasten ropes, tumbling the small boats into the water.

My family were now around me. I was very frightened – no deep-stored well of heroism manifested itself. The ship began to blow ferociously while my father explained she was signalling SOS. 'Women and children first' increased my panic and I cried out,

'I'm not leaving Daddy!'

'He'll be all right,' murmured my mother pushing me firmly in front of her and guiding me down steep companion ways into the dark bowels of the ship. We came to an opening and looked down into a life-boat. Aboard, was a seaman and a pale-faced, raincoated woman with a lidded basket at her feet. The lady, looking up at us, announced in a clear, brave voice, 'I'll take charge of the children.'

'I'm no' leavin' you,' I whispered urgently, clutching my mother and little sister.

'No – we'll keep together,' my mother replied.

Somehow we got into the lifeboat – I think I was handed down to the seaman, but I don't remember how the adults descended. Our lifeboat was loaded and the seaman rowed us away from the side of the ship. My main concern was for my father. Not even the pale-faced lady's revelation that her basket contained a puppy could take my mind off my father. Oh, the relief when at last he appeared safely in another lifeboat.

My friend, John Spence, struck up 'My Bonnie lies over the ocean' as to and fro we sailed about, not too near the bellowing ship for fear she would fall on top of us, and not too far from her for fear of being run down by other shipping in that dense blanket of fog that enfolded us.

At last somebody said, 'Here's a motor boat', and between the blasts of the *Ola*'s siren, we could make out the approaching chug, chug of an engine. Then out of the mist it finally appeared.

We were all passed down into the boat's enclosed cabin. The engine had been shut off, and we rocked and swayed on the swell. It didn't take long of that before I opened my mouth to be sick. With great presence of mind, a boy, only a year or two older than me, who was – to my mind very bravely – travelling alone, tossed a handful of pandrops into my mouth. The shock had the desired effect, and I did not disgrace myself completely.

At last we were landed on the pier at St Margaret's Hope, where kind friends, Mr and Mrs Mainland, welcomed us to their home for the weekend. The Hope folk smilingly called us 'the ship-wrecked mariners' and the pale-faced lady called her puppy 'Hunda' after the island on which we'd run aground.

From that weekend in 'the Hope', two other memories remain in my mind. Small events, but ones which mean so much to me. For the one and only time in my life I witnessed the making of sausages, courtesy of Mrs Mainland, the butcher's wife, and my child's eyes grew wide in wonder when, for the first time, I saw splashed along the curving banks that bordered the road to the pier, foxgloves, and thought they belonged to storyland.

For years I thought that St Margaret's Hope, the name of South Ronaldsay's village, had had something to do with the sad and fatal journey of the child princess, Margaret, 'Maid of Norway', who died en route to be wed to the son of Edward I of England. This is not so. St Margaret's Hope – hope meaning 'haven' – was named after a chapel built there and dedicated to St Margaret of Scotland, Saxon queen of Malcolm Canmore.

I had visited 'the Hope' before the *St Ola*'s misadventure when my beloved grandmother and I had spent a holiday with a dear, jolly, rosy-cheeked, plump little woman whom we knew fondly as 'Maric'. Mary Mackenzie, to use her proper name, lived in a cottage called 'The Lookout' which stood on a hill a few miles out of the village. Maric took us along paths that wound across grassy, buttercupped fields down to the shops in The Hope where she always bought me a thin, wrapped strap of some sort of delicious toffee-like sweet.

'May' – my name for my grandmother – and I slept in a white-painted attic room reached by climbing a wooden ladder. A girl called Sheila came from a nearby farm to play each day, and we picked plump purple blaeberries that grew in profusion in a lane stretching away from the cottage to unknown places. Our purple-stained mouths told where much of our harvest ended, but we also filled pretty cosmetic jars with berries and seeds off grasses to become stock for our 'shop'. The jars had been left by Maric's visiting sister, Violet, and in my mind I visualised this flower's namesake as someone tall, elegant, peachy complexioned and smelling as fragrant as her empty jars.

Maric's garden, full of sweet-scented, old-fashioned flowers, was a place of delight to me. As the sun set red in the western sky I used to stand by the rickety wooden fence and gaze at sad, sunken ships heeled over drunkenly in blood-red water. They reminded me of Turner's 'The Fighting Temeraire' which I used to view tearfully in one of my great-uncle's art books and sometimes I also had a 'peedie greet' for those poor broken ships below Maric's garden. Once they'd sailed proudly and people had cared for them, even loved them. It was a sad sight.

I was told that those wrecks were 'the block ships' but it was much later before I learned what this meant. They were ships sunk in the First World War to prevent intruders entering Scapa Flow, the Royal Navy's harbourage. Alas, during the Second World War, on 14 October, 1939, a daring and skilful German U-boat commander – Lieutenant Commander Prien, outwitted the barrier of block ships. Courageously he manoeuvred his submarine through a narrow, dangerous channel between the blockade and the shore, entered Scapa Flow and sank the *Royal Oak*. The submarine made its escape, leaving a weight of sadness hanging over Kirkwall that day as we mourned for the young sailors who had perished with their great ship.

Winston Churchill was not having any more of that. He ordered Scapa Flow to be sealed off securely with barriers built across the tide-harassed sounds. People muttered that it was impossible, nothing would withstand the powerful tides that raced through those channels. However, employing Italian prisoners of war, barriers were built. Thousands and thousands of steel-mesh bags were filled with boulders, swung into place by a Blondin and dumped one by one into the water until the channel was blocked. Then enormous, five- and ten-ton concrete blocks were tumbled in, on top and on either side of the rubble to secure a stout, stony barricade, and so the waters were stemmed. A road was laid along the top of the Churchill Barriers, as they were called, and so the south isles of Lamb's Holm, Glimps Holm, Burray and South Ronaldsay were, strictly speaking, no longer islands because they were now linked by causeways to Orkney's largest island, Mainland. The link was made at the village of St Mary's in the parish of Holm, pronounced Ham, and once addressed by me, I blush to remember, as the latter on an envelope.

Part of the labour force, the Italian prisoners-of-war, were detained on Lamb's Holm, the nearest island to Holm. Among those prisoners were artists and skilled craftsmen, and in their leisure hours they transformed two nissen huts into a beautiful chapel. From old tins they fashioned ornate light holders and from other scraps of metal they made a screen to divide the altar area from the main body of the chapel.

I was delighted to learn that some of their metal scraps were salvaged from the old forsaken block ships. At least some parts of them lived on in a beautiful form. The painters amongst the prisoners painted a religious scene on the wall above the altar and now when one enters the cool, shadowy building, especially for the first time, the painting with its rich, vibrant colours takes one's breath away, so unexpected is it in this humble edifice. In this quiet, brooding air, saturated with devotion and awe, you feel you have to whisper.

five

We also enjoyed holidays on the Mainland of Orkney but at that time travel overland was not the easy business of taking the car out of the garage and setting off as it is for practically everybody today. Day jaunts to the country or to visit relatives had to be planned well in advance, and motor hirers' charges of sixpence a mile tut-tutted over.

At last the great day would arrive, and a shining, high, roomy, beautifully upholstered motorcar with little take-down chairs unfolding from the backs of the front seats for the smaller members of the party, drew up at the door, along with its driver, who was also hired for the day. I always felt it was a pity we had to have this stranger in the midst of our family outings. I'm sure the driver was also uncomfortable. For part of the day, depending on the weather, he either sat in his vehicle or lolled on the grass beside it, until one of our family would go and invite him to join us for the meal. Then, awkwardly and shyly, he'd approach the picnic or join us at the table, shuffle into a place and partake of the feast in a rather embarrassed fashion, not sure whether to take part in the conversation or not.

A favourite picnic spot was the beach of gritty, silver sand and huge, smooth, scoured boulders at the Bay of Skaill. Glassily blue, white-crested breakers curled up, crashed down and frothed, hissing, up the beach from the Atlantic Ocean. Timidly I'd paddle along the foaming edge of water until the picnic was ready and I'd run to join in the meal, safe on the short-turfed links above the beach.

Nearby was the fascinating Stone Age village from the time of the first Orcadians. What a find Skarabrae must have been! Hidden through the ages until a storm blasted away the sand of centuries to reveal a cluster of squarish, corbelled-cornered, roofless stone houses. Inside were the remains of stone beds and dressers, even the seats, encircling stone hearths in the middle of the floors, were made of stone, and square stone tanks – Stone Age fridges – kept the shellfish fresh until the next meal.

It seems to me that it was only on much later visits to Skara Brae that I visited a museum there, and saw the bone pins which had been used to hold in place the animal-skins worn by the Stone Age people, and the sinew-strung bone beads they added as decoration or charms to their ensembles. The caretaker told of a broken necklace being found in a street, and surmised that it might have been left lying there because, when it broke and spilled to earth, its owner was in flight from some enemy.

I always wished I could run through the winding alleyways and enter the houses and touch the things those people of the distant past had touched. Imagine holding a necklace that had been round the warm neck of a Stone Age woman, or a crude pot Stone Age hands had formed with difficulty, or a flint scraper that had patiently cleaned the skins for clothing and the bone needle that a Stone Age woman had probably pricked her finger on when sewing together the garments. But of course my sense of touch had to be denied, and it would never do to let children explore the village, however tempting its child-sized streets, doorways and small stone houses are.

Sometimes we asked our driver to pause when we came across an unexpected sight, like the tomb of Maeshowe. Well do I remember how anxious I was to withdraw from the chill darkness. The guide's flickering candles did little to reassure me that it was quite permissible to intrude on this resting place of the dead. I felt too uneasy to appreciate the carved dragon with sword plunged through its back or the other axe incised drawings and messages left by marauding Norsemen who broke into the tomb as they passed through Orkney about 1151 on a pilgrimage to the Holy Land. We'll never know what they found and possibly removed from Maeshowe.

This round, chambered cairn is considered the finest specimen of a megalithic tomb in Britain. Adults have to bend almost double to pass through the 36-foot long, 3-foot wide entrance passage which measures about 4 foot 6 inches in height.

I felt quite claustrophobic throughout my visit and my ill at ease was heightened by the realisation that I was standing in a building of stones superbly constructed by people of the dim and distant past. I was encased in a circular mound of earth, breathing beside stalls where the dead had lain.

A more cheerful visit, though again I felt like an intruder, was to the oldest, inhabited house where some members of the resident family sat beside the fire in the middle of the stone-flagged floor. Prying tourists viewed their ancient form of heating with its hole in the roof – not directly above the fire – through which the smoke could meander. I was intrigued by how the 'skyle board' was moved by means of a long pole to encourage the smoke out of the hole. One young Canadian was much amused when, during his visit, the family's dog lifted its leg at the stone block against which the fire lay. He told his story in Canada with great glee, and to the chagrin of his Orcadian wife, who was to complain to me later of how he always omitted to point out that this occurrence only happened once and only in one rather extraordinary dwelling in Orkney. It is only to be imagined what his Canadian friends thought of our standards of hygiene after his anecdote!

Another stop was made to walk wonderingly round the Ring of Brodgar and among the Standing Stones of Stenness – both thought to have been erected by Stone Age folk. Those giant monoliths in their mysterious circles on lonely moorland cannot but fill with awe a human being so puny and insignificant beside them. There are many theories as to their purpose. Some people think they were of religious significance;

some suggest that they were of more practical use, measuring the time by the angle of the sun's rays and so were used as clocks or calendars; others maintain they were of astronomical importance. Nobody really knows.

Those day trips gave me only tantalising glimpses of what life in the rural areas was like. I enjoyed very much the little I experienced, but far more satisfactory were the country holidays lasting a blessed fortnight or so. The earliest and possibly the best of those took place in the West Mainland parish of Sandwick.

When I was between two and five it took ages to travel from Kirkwall to Sandwick. It seemed we spent all day in the rocking, rambling bus, guided over the twisting, turning, tiring miles by a remote, dark-coated figure at the front known as Mr Banks. I was always sick and totally miserable on the sagging, spring-protruding seats, regretting over and over that we had ever ventured out into this unfriendly territory.

At long last my mother dismounted (my father, because of his business, had to come later) and I, with assistance, unloaded myself, finding with amazement that I was able to totter the along the sun-drenched roadway now that the world had stopped rolling about.

Roads were not the dull, drab, tarred expanses they are nowadays. They had knobbles all over them; bits that glittered in the light like jewel dust with soft, fine powdery swathes by the flower-filled and scented ditches. There was a house near a junction and three girls with red-gold hair had grouped by the gable end, watching us walk past. They smiled shyly, but I don't remember them utter any sound.

At last, after miles of road, we arrived at a big farmhouse, low and sprawling beside the road. With my heart beating rapidly, I tip-toed past the pungent midden, fearful of any feathered, squawking creatures that might jump out at the next turn; of woufing dogs that might tumble and bound from the steading; but, most of all, in terror of the large, lumpy woman with a round, pale-moon face, dark glasses and a black shawl wrapped tight round her shoulders which she clutched with a large bony hand at the neck. At any moment she might come out of the house and screech at us, laughing maniacally, witch-like. She was the shadow that hovered over my Sandwick holidays.

More tired than ever now, we still had to climb paths the colour of burnt sienna, paths which twisted up the hill behind the witch's farm through a sea of purple-blue lupins. Always there were green plovers 'pee-witting' plaintively as they whirled and dived desperately. Perplexed yet enthralled, how I wished we could assure them that we were nothing to be afraid of.

Near the top of the hill we waded out of the gentle-smelling purple waves and there, like the ark beached above the waters, rested the stony, flag-roofed cottage of Bu's Breck.

Maggie, my mother's cousin, lived here with her son, Harry, and nephew, Peter, and far back in my memory of earliest visits there seems to me to have been a large, friendly collie, with thick orange-brown and white fur, called 'Oliver' and two cats – 'Beauty' was a tortoise-shell and her longer haired companion was known appropriately as 'Fluff'.

Maggie was tall and thin and straight with a long, ivory-white face and calm blue eyes that could sparkle into life when something hollered into her ear – for she was very deaf – appealed to her sense of humour. Her rich, chestnut hair was drawn softly back from her face and clustered in luxuriously thick plaited coils at the nape of her long, slender neck. I never remember her in any colour. She always wore widowed black, occasionally relieved by a white edging or frill and perhaps adorned with a simple brooch or pin.

Harry was a tall, lean, but sturdy boy, his face bronzed and freckled, his corn-gold hair bleached by the sun. He was always kind, considerate and well-mannered, and I never remember him speak to me in anything but a soft, kind, patient voice. I was very fond of him.

Peter had dark curly hair and small dark-blue eyes set in a crinkly, impish face. He was much older than Harry – I suppose what would now be referred to as a teenager – and gave the impression of returning home from a more sophisticated and exciting existence whose secrets he kept to himself for later when he would laugh readily, loud and long – or was it at us and our simpler ways? To me, he was master of the melodeon and fiddle and I remember wishing 'The Bonnie Lass o' Bonnacord' would go on forever.

We slept in the 'ben' end of the but and ben. There was an enormous ewer and wash-basin on a table. There was also a large, box-shaped object out of which at regular intervals every day Maggie drew a huge tray of eggs – each one marked with a neat, black dot – and deftly turned every one. This was her chicken incubator.

In a glass-fronted cupboard were displayed delicate Chinese tea-sets which had been sent home by Maggie's young sailor husband. I was very sad when I looked at them, knowing he had died long ago. One set of wide, shallow cups were of golden china decorated with Oriental scenes, their handles twisted green dragons.

The 'but' end, the kitchen-cum-living-room-cum-boys'-bedroom-when-guests-were-in-the-house end, was a cosy, comfortable place. A black stove warmed us and cooked delicious meals and baked feather-light scones.

A large, squat, brown corduroy chair, which could be changed into a bed, stood on one side of the stove. There was just room for a child to squeeze between it and the broad sill of the small, gable-end window. Crammed into this niche one day, I was happily crayoning in my book when I suddenly realised I was not alone. A fat, brown hen was in the chair. Trapped, I screamed. The hen did her best to imitate and held her ground. More screams and fierce squawks ensued, and seemed to go on and on before deliverance came and the feathered foe was forcibly routed. Maggie explained this hen had taken to laying her daily egg on the chair.

By the back wall stood a dark dresser on which were ranged dark-blue, willow-patterned plates. Never did food taste better than off these dishes when I came into the shadowy kitchen from the glaring, sun-washed hillside where I played the hours away. Nobody told me the willow pattern story and I didn't ask if there was one, but I was always fascinated by the dark-blue pictures.

The only other dish I remember was a glistening primrose-yellow egg-cup. The memories it conjures do not belong to those summer days, but to a winter night when the oil-lamp was lit. We sat on the hard, upright wooden chairs round the table and I was mesmerised by the sunshiny egg-cup. Then from out of the cold and the dark came screeches. For one moment I sat frozen in my chair. Maggie, noticing my expression, murmured, 'It's Lizzie.' I nodded but in terror I scrambled down from my chair and scuttled madly through the dark, narrow passage, past the outside door and into the dimly lit bedroom to crouch, shaking, till that fearsome visitor at long last took her leave.

Sometimes my mother would coax me through to brave it out and I would try to persuade myself Lizzie was just an old lady and make friendly overtures – showing her dolls and so on – but I never ever overcame my fear of her.

Strange to say, I do not remember her at all on our visits – working visits for Maggie – to the farm at the bottom of the hill. There in the large pale-green distempered kitchen I would watch as Maggie would remove the cream from the milk in the shiny 'separator' and then turn the clanking wooden churn to make the golden butter. All the while, an old woman huddled by the open hearth where a big, black pot dangled on a chain.

A more distant visit we made was to another farm miles across the fields. There I met a jolly, laughing family – a mother, two grown-up sons and two grown-up daughters. In the early evening the herd of 'milkers' clattered past the back door into the byre and each member of the family seized a milking stool and got into position beside them. Then the white milk squirted and hissed into the pails. As a treat, I was given a glass of milk warm from the cow, but all the way home on Harry's sympathetic back I groaned and squealed with stomach pains.

No doubt Auntie Jessie was told all about this on her next visit to us. She was Maggie's aunt and walked miles over the fields to see us and bring dripping golden honeycombs straight from her son Jamie's kept bees. I never hear of 'a land flowing with milk and honey' without thinking of Auntie Jessie and Jamie. From her talk of 'de loch, de fishin'' and de owld colonel', I gathered that their far-off home was very different from ours at Bu's Breck.

As in all lives set against the backdrop of Orkney, the sea must play its part. We could not see or hear it from Bu's Breck, but I remember one lamp-lit night in the kitchen when we sat in a close group on the hard wooden chairs and passed from head to head a pair of heavy headphones to listen to boats blowing in the New Year on the wireless.

Then there was a bright, breezy day when we went to a distant beach where deep-blue water heaved into white-crested breakers that charged in and fumed and frothed on the sand. Here a big man led Maggie out into the rolling water and her black form fell backwards and disappeared beneath the swaying sea. At length, she reappeared and with the man waded ashore dripping wet. Then, oh horror, it was Harry's turn. To the knot of people on the beach it was just an ordinary Brethren baptism but to a small child the whole thing was a terrible experience never to be forgotten.

One summer not long ago I took my husband and children to Bu's Breck. A very interested, friendly farmer let us walk by his steading and opened the gate at the bottom of a gently sloping field – for that was all the hill now was. Not a lupin was left; rough grass had taken over, no doubt, following the merciless plough-share.

We came to the cottage. It had hardly any roof left intact and seemed such a small and shrunken shell I could hardly see how we had all fitted in it more than fifty years ago. But as I stood inside the crumbling walls I could visualise the velvet chair and the dark-blue willow-patterned dishes. I could hear the notes of the fiddle and I could feel again the atmosphere of warmth and love that surrounded me in that house.

six

When Harry left school, Maggie decided they should move nearer the town so that he could follow a trade, and so that they would be nearer the Brethren Hall in Kirkwall. She bought a long, low house called 'Cot o' Blinkbonny' in the district known as 'Scapa', which bordered the west edge of Scapa Flow. Neither I nor Beauty the tortoiseshell wholly approved of this move. Indeed, Beauty showed her disapproval by returning the ten miles or so to 'Bu's Breck' where old neighbours spotted her living the independent life of a wild cat.

Now only approximately three miles separated Maggie and my family in Kirkwall, and often she, as always completely clothed in black from brimmed felt hat to pointed toes, cycled sedately into town to see us, to visit the bank and cash her 'egg cheque'. With 'Blinkbonny' she had bought a few acres of land and, scattered over these, were her neat, white wooden hen-houses from the inmates of which she made her living.

On high days and holidays we'd walk the three or so hilly miles to 'Cot o' Blinkbonny' where the most delicious meals and home-baked scones and cakes awaited us. Most of our visits took place when the walled garden at the back of the house was full of gaily coloured flowers, and along its side ran a burbling summer burn. Further from the house two grassy hillocks rose on either side of a green slope. To my great delight, my parents, my sister and I were sometimes invited to spend a week or two at this idyllic spot. Hours were whiled away paddling about in the burn's amber water. Dozens of pairs of knickers were dyed irremovable green from sliding on our bottoms down the sides of the hillocks until our mother sacrificed her old leather coat to be a 'sledge' for our sport.

Sometimes we walked some miles southwards from 'Cot o' Blinkbonny' into the neighbouring parish of Orphir where my grandfather was cutting his peats on the miles of heather-covered moors. Near his peat bank we boiled our kettle and picnicked on the sweet-scented heather while larks sang, bees buzzed and butterflies fluttered around us. After the picnic we usually tramped over the moorland to a sheltered, bracken-filled valley called 'The Bught'. Someone once told me this name meant 'the sheep-fold', but I don't know if this is true or not. On our way, we passed the one-roomed Scapa School. Little did I think that one day I'd teach in that building and make the lunch-time cocoa for my twenty eight pupils, who represented every class from the Baby Class, now called Primary One, right up to the Qualifying Class now known as Primary Seven.

A traditional family celebration with the 'Blinkbonny' household was a mid-day dinner on New Year's Day – though my grandmother always liked to know the progress of 'The Ba'' before leaving town. Both she and her two brothers took a keen, lively interest in the games of 'The Ba'' which were held every Christmas Day and New Year's Day.

Kirkwall has been a 'divided' town since the twelfth century, when Orkney was a Norse earldom. From the Cathedral to the south – 'up the street' – was 'The Laverock' where the Bishop ruled. If you lived 'down the street' – from the Cathedral to the sea – you were an Earl's man. The two factions were called 'Up-the-gates' and 'Down-the-gates', 'gates' meaning roads or streets, and over the years the appellations became shortened to 'Uppies' and 'Doonies'.

A ball game, originally one in which the ball was only kicked, was held between the two parts of the town every New Year's Day. By and by, the games multiplied and there was a 'Boys' Ba'' in the mornings of Christmas Day and New Year's Day followed by the 'Men's Ba'' in the afternoons. The form of the game changed, too. As had always been the way, someone – perhaps a woman – threw the ball into the air at the Market Cross in front of the Cathedral as the great clock in the minster struck the hour. On the street below the Market Green, the Uppies and Doonies in their oldest clothes and sturdiest boots waited to seize the ba', but not necessarily to kick it for, the game being totally without rules, anything could be done with the ba'.

They surged together – a heaving, pushing scrum from which clouds of steam rose in the crisp, frosty air – and they went on struggling and striving, forcing and sometimes fighting, for hours and hours.

The Uppies tried with all their might to make their way, bearing the ball with them, to their territory 'up the street'. I always understood their goal to be 'the owld castle' – an ancient looking corner of a stone wall where the street met two roads. The Doonies put all their strength and stamina into forcing their way 'down the street' to the freezing cold, often stormy waters by the shore into which they hurled the ball. One of their number then plunged into the sea and retrieved the trophy so establishing a 'Doonie' victory.

Onlookers who had only come to watch often could not resist adding their weight to their side, and sometimes were absorbed in The Ba', willy-nilly, best suits and all. Barricaded premises stood the strain as best they could as the weighty mass fell and strained against them. Flesh was bruised black and bones were cracked many a time, but enthusiasm for the game and determination to win never waned.

You were born an Uppie or a Doonie. If your place of birth was above the Market Cross you were a life-time Uppie, and if you came into the world below the Market Cross you were a Doonie forever.

My mother's family were staunch Doonies. So it was unintentionally obliging of my father to arrive at Kirkwall Pier all those years ago and gain automatic admission to their side. Reaching the islands by Scapa pier or, in later years, by Grimsetter aerodrome, marked you an Uppie.

Twice – once in the Boys' game and once in the Men's – my Great-uncle Johnny had swum for the ba', and played the game throughout so well that the assembled players, as was the custom, voted him the winner of the ba' itself. His trophies – beautiful, shiny, polished spheres composed of segments of brown and blackened leather stitched securely together and packed firmly with cork so that they could float – were among his proudest possessions.

The spirits of my grandmother and great-uncles see-sawed throughout Christmas Day and New Year's Day with the movement of the ba'. Great was the rejoicing when the news arrived – 'the ba's doon', but, oh, the gloom and shaking of heads and doleful comparisons with the days of their youth if the Uppies won.

One summer interlude at 'Cot o' Blinkbonny' was interrupted by a sudden, hectic dash into Kirkwall. My mother fairly dirled the old pram containing my sister over the miles while I skipped and ran alongside. Her goal was Brandyquoy Park, lying above Earl's Palace in Kirkwall. Here a dress rehearsal was to take place that day for the pageant to mark the octo-centenary of St Magnus Cathedral.

My mother was determined not to miss this special occasion, and was anxious that we children experience it, too. I'm pretty certain I didn't realise it was the history of my homeland I was witnessing, but even though its true significance escaped me, I felt moved by the scenes I saw, and not only experienced my first theatre, but also my first yearnings to take part in drama.

White-robed Druids presided beside an altar towards which a struggling girl with beautiful, long, golden-brown hair was being dragged. I knew enough about altars to realise she was about to be sacrificed, and sat with a lump in my throat wondering wildly why my mother had brought us to witness such a horrible event. Surely something would prevent it? But no, she was laid on the altar and secured there. Then, in the nick of time, a solemn procession of monks, with cross uplifted, appeared. The Druids fell back in awe as the cross approached, the sacrificial victim was released, the pagan people worshipped, and I privately thanked the miracle worker of Galilee. No divine intervention, however, cheered me when the good Earl Magnus knelt before Earl Hakon's cook to receive his death blow, and I longed to warn poor Lady Thora, mother of the murdered earl, that her party to welcome back her son and his cousin was to end in disaster.

A gauze-like fence divided 'the stage' from the ruins of the Earl's Palace and I seem to remember a shadowy long-ship glide along behind it. Maybe this was Earl Paul's galley setting out for a battle off Tankerness in which he defeated Olvir Rosta; or Earl Rognvald's ship waiting to take him from Norway to Orkney to wrest his uncle Magnus' share of the earldom from Earl Paul; or the vessel that in 1151 took him and his Crusader companions to the Holy Land. I don't know, for only three out of the eight scenes remain in my mind. I have read that Scene Two portrayed the dedication of Earl Thorfinn's Christ's Church in Birsay. I have read, too, that Scene Seven was set in Fair Isle, and showed Uni, Rognvald's saboteur, putting paid to anybody being able to start off Earl Paul's warning system by lighting the first beacon.

However, no one seems to have written about the part of the pageant I recall most vividly. As the scenes on stage were changed, a pair of living curtains closed to hide the activity from the audience. The curtains were composed of two lines of girls with wide yellow skirts so designed that one side of each skirt was held up, I think attached to a pole, to touch the neighbouring girl, and so give the effect and do the work of a curtain. How I longed to be one of the little girls at the ends.

Brandyquoy Park was a well-chosen site for this historical celebration, for, looking forwards and skywards from the auditorium, the scene on the back-cloth consisted of a cluster of Kirkwall's historic buildings – the Earl's Palace, the Bishop's Palace and St Magnus Cathedral itself.

The Earl's Palace was built circa 1600 by Patrick Stewart and is considered possibly the finest example of secular Renaissance architecture in Scotland. Patrick's father, Robert Stewart, illegitimate son of James V of Scotland, was made Earl of Orkney in 1581. His reign is reputed to have been one of oppression and tyranny. It was said that he cheated his tenants by altering the Norse weights and measures by which the amount of rent, paid in kind, was calculated; that there was no justice for the living or for the dead, since he threw people into prison or even sentenced them to death without allowing them to be tried, and even put the deceased on trial, charging them with real or trumped up offences and then, finding them guilty, seized their possessions from their heirs. Ships were no longer free to cross the Pentland Firth at will in case any traveller should tell what was going on in Orkney. Free people were forced to work for the Earl with no recompense. Lands were grabbed from their rightful owners and given to the Earl's supporters.

Robert's son, Patrick, followed in his father's footsteps, twisting the law, even making laws to suit his whims and, according to *The New Orkney Book,* going as far as to destroy *The Law Book of Orkney* and the *Records of Kirkwall.* However, a recent history of Orkney points out that the evidence for the Stewarts' misrule was in fact provided by their enemies and as no evidence in their favour was ever recorded, the reliability of this evidence is, at best, uncertain.

At any event, Bishop Law apparently got word through to James VI of Scotland who had Earl Patrick removed, so ending the reign of the Stewart Earls. But not the story, for it is said that, though the Earl had led an almost regal weekly procession to worship in the Cathedral, with an accompaniment of fifty musketeers, guards and a bevy of other gentlemen, his execution in Edinburgh had to be postponed till he learned to say the Lord's Prayer. His end finally came on 6 February, 1615.

Bishop Law was paid handsomely for his trouble, taking over the Earl's magnificent palace shortly after its completion. We can imagine how Patrick felt about that.

Now in ruins, the Bishop's Palace must have been a grand building in its day. During the time of Bishop Robert Reid (1541–58) it was extensively rebuilt and it was he who erected the 'Moosie Tooer', the round tower that is the most impressive bit of the ruin. Poor Bishop Reid, returning from France where he'd attended the wedding of Mary Queen of Scots to the Dauphin, died at Dieppe on his way home. Three of his companions also expired and poison was suspected. Bishop Reid had been interested in education, providing money for the Grammar School in Kirkwall and founding Edinburgh University. A little statue in a wall niche on the town side of the 'Moosie Tooer' is said to be the effigy of this bishop.

It was in the Bishop's Palace that the defeated King Hakon of Norway lay dying after the Battle of Largs in 1263. I've often imagined the sick king, lying in the cold, draughty palace set about by Orkney's persistent, battering gales that howl and whistle and buffet on for days at a time. He passed the long hours of the dark, winter nights by first listening to readings in Latin, and later, as his body became too weak and his mind too weary to be bothered with a foreign language, by having read to him the stories of the saints and the sagas of the kings of Norway in his native Norse.

King Hakon's life ended just after midnight on 15 December, 1263. His body rested in the Cathedral of St Magnus till spring came, when his large, proud, oaken warship, with its gilded dragons' heads fore and aft, bore him back to Norway.

One of the Norwegian dignitaries, the Bishop of Nidaros, who had come to join in the octo-centenary celebrations, presented Kirkwall with a statue of St Olaf as a gift from his cathedral. A twin statue was to be erected in Nidaros Cathedral, in Trondheim, which had been built about the same time as the Cathedral of St Magnus and displaying the same Norman-Gothic architecture. The presentation was made at a service in the cathedral in which the statue now stands.

James III of Scotland, in about 1486, presented the cathedral to the town of Kirkwall, so, though the Church of Scotland holds regular services in the Cathedral of St Magnus it belongs neither to church nor state, but to the people of Kirkwall.

After the pageant, we returned to Scapa, our play in the burn or on the grassy hillocks echoing the scenes of times past. On occasion, we were interrupted by our mother deciding to take us what seemed like miles across fields to the shores of Scapa Flow. There in uncomfortable elasticated blue swimming costumes we bathed happily for a short time and then, complaining as the novelty of the exercise wore off, we turned almost as blue as our garments with cold. No matter, our indomitable mother, after her efforts to get us to the beach, refused to let us curtail the bathing time she'd decreed.

I always thought this stony shore should have had a name other than 'Scapa'. When we were in town our parents talked of 'gan oot tae Scapa', they were referring to a beach of soft, creamy-coloured sands, green, grassy banks sprinkled liberally with pale, yellow primroses, and a small, sturdy pier. However, when the Orcadian singer, Angus Findlater sang 'Lonely Scapa Flow', written by another Orcadian, Ally Windwick, it was the expanse of untamed sea stretching from the beach below Blinkbonny that I envisaged.

The song recalls the time when the ships of the Royal Navy rode at anchor among the south isles of Orkney, and watchers on the shore looked across the evening waters at their rocking, swaying lights and listened to their distant bugles sounding.

The streets of Kirkwall would then be enlivened by the presence of young sailors so attractive in their navy blue and white that many pretty heads were turned and many hearts beat a little faster. Midshipmen in civilian suits and pork-pie hats marched in and out of Cromwell's Road. I see them striding along in long lines abreast, as they often did, taking the road before them, wielding arrogant walking sticks, braying in loud, plumy public-school voices and emanating an air of pseudo superiority which such educational establishments seem to breed.

It was not till 1812 that the Admiralty's attention was drawn to the natural anchorage of Scapa Flow, almost land-locked by the South Isles of Orkney. By 1914 the Navy realised its worth. It was large enough to accommodate a fleet of sufficient strength to patrol and keep open the vital northern sea-route between Scotland and Norway when Germany threatened our country. Again, in the Second World War, Scapa Flow was the northern base for the Royal Navy from which watch was kept on Germany's routes to the Atlantic.

Germany's navy, too, entered Scapa Flow. Proud ships, captured at the end of the First World War when their country was defeated, they could not bear their humiliation and one fateful day, scuttled by their skeleton crews, they plunged down into their watery grave. There the German fleet rested undisturbed for some years until a salvage firm set about raising them, only to tow them away to be sold as scrap metal. *The Man who bought a Navy* was written about Mr Cox of the salvage firm, Cox and Danks.

The last ship to be raised, upside down, as were so many others, was the *Derfflinger*. The living quarters of a salvage crew was perched on her bottom. A member of this uniquely lodged group came to the meetings of the Brethren in Kirkwall, and I'm afraid the romance of his situation interested me more than his preaching.

A thousand years earlier, Skalpeid or *isthmus*, meaning 'a ship', the Norse name for Scapa, was valued as a place of rest and shelter. We read in the *Orkneyinga Saga* not only about Norse long-ships and barges speeding to and fro or anchoring in Scapa waters, but also about some of the people who settled in Scapa Flow's vicinity. Its history is more turbulent than its sheltered waters, but to my mind it is a place where you can stand quietly and remember those who lived and died by this now lonely expanse of sea.

seven

My mother's taking us to see the octo-centenary pageant would no doubt have been frowned upon by many of the Brethren. Having started her religious career as a member of the Salvation Army, she was more broad-minded than most of the Brethren.

When, at long last, I was of age to be taken to Sunday School in the bare, upper room in Victoria Street what an anti-climax it was. I don't know what I expected, but it certainly wasn't what I found. My father had always talked about going to Sunday School as though it was going to be a great treat. I got as far as visualising an enormous, barn-like red door, but could not imagine the delights to be experienced within.

In reality, the door was not even red, and certainly not broad, but narrow and a gloomy green. Coconut matting covered a narrow stairway that led up to a brown-grained door, the entrance to a hall with an uncovered, wooden floor, walls wood-lined halfway up (the top half being distempered in cream), and the only touch of decoration being a stencilled brown pattern along the edge where wood and distemper met. A plain, varnished wooden table on which stood a plain, varnished wooden desk faced the congregation's plain, varnished wooden forms.

We, the Sunday School pupils, were divided according to age and sex into classes, each class grouped around a teacher. My first group was seated at the back of the hall with a small, curly-haired woman whose sweet voice, Sunday after Sunday, told us: 'For God so loved the world that He gave His only begotten Son that whosoever believeth in Him shall not perish but hath everlasting life.' We chanted this after her, her sole bit of teaching, until it was committed to memory, and our efforts were rewarded with a sweetie.

Everlasting life was of prime importance. This short 'sojourn in the vale of tears' merited little attention. Indeed, no matter how worthily you behaved on earth it counted as nothing. Good works could not ensure a place in Heaven. But, before the eternal bliss came death. Thoughts of dying shadowed my living all the days of my childhood and youth. How I prayed my loved ones would be spared after I said my 'bonie-words' at night. My grandmother, May, knelt beside my bed while I chanted solemnly:

This night as I lie down to sleep,
I give Thee Lord my soul to keep.
If I should die before I wake,
I pray Thee Lord my soul to take.

Then came the names of our household for whose souls I pleaded. And so with thoughts of dying uppermost in my mind I obeyed May – 'Lie doon noo, buddo,' – but usually for some time could not oblige and 'go tae sleep'.

I confided to my mother how I could not bear the thought that one of our family might be taken from us. When Nanny, my great-grandmother, eventually died at the age of 96 the experience was every bit as dreadful as I had feared, and people assuring me that she was now happy in Heaven with Jesus or that God had taken her 'home' only made me feel rebellious towards such inconsiderate deities.

My mother declared stoutly that we were not thinking of dying. We were expecting Jesus to come back when we'd all be caught up to meet him in the air. My mother expected this to happen soon – any day now, it seemed – and though it was a cheering idea in some ways, I felt bound to admit to her that I did not join her in wishing for its imminence as I'd rather like to grow up, get married and have children.

'We-ell,' she admitted grudgingly, 'I suppose that's only natural.'

Wakening in the silent hours of night I used to sit up in bed panic stricken, with rapidly beating heart, straining my ears for some human sound, for it was so quiet I feared Jesus had come and everybody else in the household had been caught up and was away. I was never sure I was properly 'saved' or 'born again' as they described the conversion of a doomed, hell-bound sinner to a Christian. I couldn't remember a time when I hadn't believed what I was told was necessary to be 'saved', but there had been no definite moment of conversion which I was told had to take place. I worried myself sick about this.

My hope of being saved existed alongside my fear of it as to be saved meant more than admission to heaven. It meant I had to endure something of which I was absolutely terrified. So I dreaded the usual questioning of visiting evangelists. 'Is this little girl saved?' they would ask and then, after my father had assured them I was, 'So she knows the next step.' If I hadn't already been crying, then this last statement would have caused torrents of tears to flow down my cheeks as well I knew that the 'next step' meant the horror of baptism; a ceremony which had haunted me since I had first witnessed it all those years ago.

'Sin' was a frequently used word. What was it, I wondered. Bad actions, bad words and if you didn't actually do or say anything bad you could be sure you had sinned by thinking bad thoughts. I was sure I didn't *ask* for any bad thoughts. Thoughts came into my mind unbidden and before I could stop them. Then there was that pesky man Adam in the garden. Because he had sinned, you, being his descendant, were born a sinner. There was no way out of the fix. We were left in no doubt that, as my father many a time put it, 'There is a Heaven to gain; a Hell to shun'.

I found it a great relief to learn that the Devil was really a fallen angel called Lucifer, meaning 'a being of light'. So that instead of dreading the appearance in my lamp-lit bedroom of a dark, sinister-faced, horned and tailed personage whose appearance I had based on a picture in our card game of 'Pilgrim's Progress', I used to assure myself that he'd really be quite beautiful should he come to visit me.

My broad-minded mother tried to cheer things up for her Sunday School class by taking along my sister's toy ark and animals to illustrate the story of Noah. The children started to play with the wooden animals, arranging them on the form and dropping them on the floor.

'Tut-tut what a way to carry on,' snorted our stern-faced teacher, her mauve lips clipped in a thin, annoyed line of righteous disapproval, her eyes like cold pebbles regarding the scene stonily from behind her steel rimmed spectacles. Well I missed the sweet voice and nature of my previous teacher as I was torn between loyalty to my mother and the desire to keep on the right side of straight-laced authority.

Another sign of my mother's religious laxity was her giving way to my overwhelming desire to wear a Brownie uniform. I didn't know what joining the Brownies entailed, but, oh, to be one of the crowd of little girls dressed all in brown! I had hardly achieved my desire when we were told we were to take part in a Church Parade. The church we were to attend was St Magnus Cathedral. A lady in navy called 'Tony' by the Brownie Pack (which I much later realised should have been 'Tawny' for we were all pretending to belong to the owl family, a notion which completely escaped me at the time), passed on to us an extraordinary order regarding our visit to the church. 'When Brown Owl gets up, you stand.' So my best friend, Winnie, and I spent most of our time in the august minster of St Magnus, gazing up at a gallery where at any moment, we agreed in whispers, a brown owl would make its appearance.

Despite our disappointment, we proudly marched from the Cathedral, just as the Brethren were coming out of their morning meeting. I was spotted amongst the Brownies and immediately my mother found herself in hot water. She should not have allowed me to join any such worldly organisation. The self-righteous condemner boasted that neither of *her* two offspring would dream of taking such a worldly step, and had they even ventured to suggest such a thing, it would most certainly have been forbidden. My mother, in mild reply, expressed the hope that they would never do anything worse than join the Brownies.

But Brownies grow up and reach the stage where they 'fly up' to the Girl Guides. Guides danced at their parties so there was no question of a Brethren Brownie becoming a dancing Girl Guide.

The Brethren did have two annual occasions of comparative levity. There was the Sunday School Picnic in summer and the Sunday School Soiree in winter.

Sunday School picnics did not always venture far from home. Buses would drive us, singing religious choruses to a cow-patted field at 'Greenfield', a farmhouse near the end of Cromwell's Road. There we ran races, ate food out of paper bags and drank milky tea poured from kettles.

I much preferred my family's private visits to 'Greenfield' when 'the boys' – two grown-up men – showed me their egg collection arranged in many drawers in a glass-topped cabinet in the lamp-lit hall; when, from the cool kitchen, a culinary delight composed of lemons and apples, and who knows what other delectable ingredients, all topped with pale-gold meringue was brought to the large table in the living-room; when, after tea, we played 'Lexicon', and passed round the 'Promise Box'. This box was crammed full of small, upright rolls of paper and contained a pair of minute tweezers. With the tweezers each person extracted the paper roll of his or her choice and, on opening out the little roll, read aloud to the assembled company a promise to be found in the Bible. It might be, '"Lo, I am with you always, even unto the end of the world," Matthew, chapter 28, verse 20'; or '"He that spared not His own son, but delivered Him up for us all, how shall He not with Him also freely give us all things," Romans, chapter 8, verse 32'. As with horoscopes, you felt it was a message for the future just for you.

Maybe a hymn would bring the evening to a close, followed by a prayer from one of the men, while we all knelt beside our chairs. Then the servant would be summoned and told to bring the gig to the door. Home we clip-clopped behind a trotting pony, his route illuminated for him by the flickering candlelights at either side of our vehicle and by the moon and the stars above.

In contrast, 'Binscarth', a mansion house set in grounds outside the village of Finstown, provided Brethren picnickers with a field and a walk through its plantation of trees. 'Binscarth', dating from at least 1500, means 'the farm in the skarth', which was the word for a ridge in the hills. To me, the shady, treed place with its shivering, whispering leaves was the woods of story books. In such a place Red Riding Hood had wandered unwisely; Tom Thumb and brothers were left to their fate; a gingerbread house, embellished with sweetmeats had appeared, and the sad trees shed their leaves to cover those unfortunate Babes in the Wood. The plantation, for at least one Orcadian child was an alien, exciting, romantic, unusual environment. It still gives me a thrill of pleasure and excitement to lay my hands on the bark of a tree.

More adventurous were the picnics that took place over the sea. We all assembled on Kirkwall pier, our tea-mugs a-dangle, and excitedly crossed the gang-way of the *Earl Sigurd*, *Earl Thorfinn* or *Iona*, the funnel of the chartered ship busily belching black smoke as she got her steam up.

Across the choppy, blue waves we were borne, trailing behind us a churned-up furrow of sea. On one occasion our destination was the hilly island of Rousay, called *Hrolfsey* or 'Rolf's island' by the Norsemen. Rousay was the home of General Sir Frederick Burroughs, KCB, immortalised – but not to his credit – by Edwin Muir. The General lived in Westness House until the 1870s when he built a mansion and named it 'Trumland House'. The General benefited the island of Rousay by building Trumland Pier and introducing improved systems of agriculture, but, even so, Edwin Muir describes him as a bad landlord who, in a short time, drove the poet's father off his farm on the island of Wyre. It is not surprising then, that Muir took his revenge by belittling General Burroughs in poetry and prose.

In the twelfth century it was at Westness in Rousay that Earl Paul's grand-daughter, Ingibiorg Ragna, lived with her husband, Sigurd. Sigurd was a loyal, faithful friend of Earl Paul. He was in charge of the warning beacon on Rousay, one of a chain of fires arranged by Earl Paul to be lit on island after island were an enemy to approach. Unfortunately, his early warning system was known to his opponent, Earl Rognvald, who sabotaged it when he came to claim the earldom.

Earl Paul, holidaying beside his friend Sigurd of Westness, went otter hunting one morning. Sweyn Asleifson, pretending he was a merchant, and with more than half his crew hidden in their skin sleeping-bags, fooled Paul's men into telling him the Earl's whereabouts. Sweyn, with his band of thirty, then sprang ashore, killed the Earl's followers, kidnapped Earl Paul, and made off.

When the Earl did not come home to Westness, Sigurd sent out a search party who returned with news of the carnage and the disappearance of Earl Paul. Loyal Sigurd refused to bow the knee to the usurper, Rognvald, until he knew for certain what had become of Earl Paul. Eventually, Sweyn arrived in Kirkwall with the story that Earl Paul, now blinded, was going to enter a monastery and would never return. A mission was sent to Rousay to break the news to Sigurd. It was with great sadness that Sigurd heard the tale and remarked that the worst thing of all was that the Earl had been made sightless, otherwise wherever Paul was, he, Sigurd, would have gone to be with him. Anarchy and terrorism are not new phenomena.

Who fled into the circular, stone towers called 'the brochs' along Rousay's shores when alien ships appeared off-shore? It is thought they were Iron Age farmers. And some believe that Stone Age people from as early as 2000 BC laid their dead chieftains and their wives with their jewellery in the many stalled cairns excavated in Rousay.

All those places of past importance lay around us Sunday School scholars, but we knew not and neither did we care. A sunny field, a hanky to tie your leg to your partner's for the three-legged race, and a creamy cookie in your paper poke: that was all we asked of our trip to Rousay.

Not so when the *Iona* bobbed her way across the tumbling sound called 'The String' that separated the isle of Shapinsay from the Mainland. There, on the isle of Elliar Holm, stood a beautiful, white lighthouse station of special interest to my family. Once long ago, the principal lightkeeper and his wife came from that lighthouse to interview my grandmother-to-be and to invite her to become their servant maid. Her brother, Richie, wishing like the rest of her family to keep her safely at home, won her from her bid for freedom by offering the gift of a gold watch if she gave up the idea. The gold watch won the day. Life is strange in its turnings, and from my very much later experience as a lightkeeper's wife, I've often wondered how a lightkeeper, albeit a principal, could have afforded to employ a maid. Perhaps his wife was 'delicate' and not able to cope with the housework; perhaps she was not only 'delicate' but rich – lucky lightkeeper!

It was to Elwick Bay, sheltered by Elliar Holm, that the Norse king, Hakon, brought his armada of around a hundred ships in 1263. He had a tent erected on shore in Shapinsay – a temporary church – where he attended Mass and then he entertained some of the local people on his enormous, thirty-seven oared *Christ-Ship* with its gleaming, gold covered dragons' heads at bow and stern.

On arrival at the assigned field in Shapinsay, the picnic ran the usual course of events at Rousay, but before boarding the *Iona* for the sail home came a brush with Shapinsay's history.

We were permitted to parade two by two through the apple-treed, flower-filled gardens and grape-hung glasshouses of Balfour Castle. I felt my fingers itch to touch the tempting bunches as we passed but no touching was allowed.

Balfour Castle was built in 1897 by Colonel David Balfour on the site of two earlier houses – 'Cliffdale' and earlier still 'Sound'. 'Sound' had become, through marriage, a residence of James Fea, schoolfellow and captor of John Gow the pirate who left his final days of freedom on the island of Eday. It's interesting to hear something more of James Fea, though it is not a happy story. He embraced the Jacobite cause and provided arms to Prince Charles Edward Stuart's supporters in 1745. Consequently, in retaliation, the mansion of 'Sound' was set alight the following year and reduced to ashes.

Scholars of Victoria Hall Sunday School though we were, we were not admitted to the castle itself. Many years later, when Miss Balfour opened it to visitors in aid of the Red Cross, a friend and I grasped our opportunity. We were coming to the end of our short day-trip to

Shapinsay, during which we'd walked along hot, dusty roads and enjoyed a delicious lunch of bere bannock spread with Orkney farmhouse butter and accompanied by slabs of crumbly, white Orkney farmhouse cheese eaten in the parlour of one of the cottages in the island's village of Elwick. Bere bannock is a round, dark-brown scone made of ground bere meal, self-raising flour, baking soda, cream of tartar and salt, all mixed together with buttermilk and baked on a girdle set on top of the stove. Well I remember that delicious lunch and the hospitality of the lady who prepared it for us. There were no hotels, restaurants or cafes in Shapinsay in those days so, before leaving Kirkwall, my parents had told us of this villager, whose name I can't recall, but who was known to provide snacks for visitors to the island. When we found her cottage, we knocked on the door and asked if she would give us lunch. She made us very welcome and her charge can't have been extraordinary for I have no memory of it. So were affairs conducted in the days before everywhere was geared for the tourist trade.

A tall, elegant young lady admitted our dishevelled selves through the castle door. She showed us the family's treasures in various rooms and demonstrated a secret door in the library. Everything was fascinating but the occurrence on which we both commented afterwards, and the feeling it inspired which I can still recall, was when our cool, neatly dressed guide, with not a curl out of place, set her feet in their unblemished, highly polished shoes on a pure white, fluffy sheepskin rug. We immediately felt hotter, dustier and more rumpled than ever.

The other 'fun' event in Victoria Hall Sunday School's calendar was the Soiree. The climax of this occasion was reached halfway through the evening.

We'd heard the classes of boys repeat, parrot-wise, huge chunks of scripture, girls in swaying lines sing hymns and we had bawled religious choruses in unison. Some of the choruses were enlivened by hand movements. When you built your house on the rock and not upon the sand, you needn't fear the storm or the earthquake's shock – demonstrated by a mighty clap of hands. When you'd been converted – 'saved' – and in consequence, your cup of joy was overflowing, you sang 'Running over, running over' while rolling your hands round each other; 'My cup's full' – hands cupped; 'and running over' – hands rolling over each other again.

Then came teatime, the highlight of the evening, when everybody was given a paper poke of food along with a cup of tea. The feast over, formal permission was given by the chairman to blow up the paper bags, burst them, crumple them up and throw them at him. Since the chairman was my adored Daddy, I did not find this ritual the least bit amusing.

Usually the Soiree ended with a 'model lesson' by Robert Rendall who became one of Orkney's poets. Of Robert's 'models' made of wood, I can only recall one. It consisted of two hills, one representing earth, and the other representing heaven. Various bridges were inserted in order to reach heaven – bridges labelled with such worthy titles as 'Good Works' and 'Education' – but no matter how worthy, every bridge failed to close the gap until we came to one entitled 'Salvation'.

Robert's models were regarded as being rather clever, and I'm sure they were, but it is not as a preacher that I think of him. I remember him instead whenever I see clumps of red poppies, for I once grew such a clump from a packet of seeds which I'd bought with a tuppence he'd given me. I remember with mirth how at one of his parties, he and his niece, May, appeared dressed as the king and queen of Siam. Solemnly, they invited the roomful of guests to sing the National Anthem of Siam to the tune of our National Anthem. They held up a placard to show us the words and led us in singing – 'o wha ta na siam'. It was only after we had actually uttered the words that we realised exactly what we had been singing!

I fondly remember him, too, as the Robert who loved Birsay.

Birsay

Here on this rocky coast I roved, and here
Beside the sea in happy boyhood played,
Ere I had felt the bonds of ruthless trade
Or mourned time's loss through many a wasteful year.
Along these cliffs, when summer skies were clear,
I watched the waves with thunder long delayed
Break on the shore; or saw the colours fade
From evening clouds, and knew that night was near.
Here once again, where grow the wild sea-pinks,
With idle steps I go, and mind at ease
From life's mad haste. O look! The red sun sinks
In golden floods of light; and with the breeze
Comes faintly now across the grassy links
The ageless music of the rolling seas.

ROBERT RENDALL

eight

Late one summer's evening there came a knock on the door of our caravan on the Links at Birsay. My mother answered the door and there was Robert Rendall.

Robert invited my mother, my sister and myself – my father had returned to town on business – to walk with him over to the Brough of Birsay. The Brough was a little island when the tide was in, but could be reached on foot when the tide receded, leaving exposed a narrow causeway.

In the gathering dusk, we picked our way over the narrow, wet and slippery, seaweedy causeway. Robert suggested we look for 'Groatie Buckies', the local name for small, cream and pink cowrie shells. Though we were with an expert on the subject of shells – for Robert produced a book, *Mollusca Orcadensia* – we found but few.

Perhaps Robert's first encounters with the world of shells had been when, as a little boy, he learned from his mother a game that had come down through the generations, from the time of Norse dominance. In this game, domestic animals were represented by shells, and herded into a farm steading built of stones from the beach. My husband's mother had also played this game. Robert was to discover that both in Norway and Orkney there were old dialect names applied to certain shells, and those used in Orkney were derived from the Norse tongue.

Robert's collection of Orcadian shells and the title for his work which he submitted to the Proceedings of the Royal Society of Edinburgh had been prepared well in advance. His first collection grew in wooden boxes which had started life as containers for wines and chocolates. The smaller wooden chocolate-boxes became drawers which were fitted into the wine cases and the whole 'cabinet', decorated on either side with Orkney's coat of arms and paintings of sea-weed, was labelled 'Mollusca Orcadensia'.

Leaving the Brough's rocky beach, we clambered up on to the grass-covered island. A small, unmanned lighthouse was the most notable feature, but Robert opened our eyes to other places of interest at our feet. He pointed out what he took to be the remains of a monastery – the altar and the cells of the monks – from shapes that could be discerned among the shaggy turf.

Much excavation has taken place since our visit to Birsay. The iron bell of a Celtic monastery has been taken out of its stone burial cist where it had either been hidden or laid to rest as carefully as though it were a human being. The place of contemplation and worship in which it rang is thought to date from the sixth or seventh century, and to have survived till the ninth century when heathen Norsemen invaded the islands and called this islet off the Birsay shore *Brough*, meaning 'an island fortress'.

Norse farmers built their farmsteads on the ruins of the monastery, and by and by the earls who ruled Orkney decided to make Birsay their capital. A large Norse house of the eleventh century has been found. Earl Thorfinn, the Mighty, who came home from Rome about 1050 after being absolved from his sins by the Pope, built his 'Christ's Kirk' in Birsay. It is now thought that this church, later altered to become a cathedral, was on the same site as today's parish church of St Magnus, appropriately named after the earl who seemed to haunt the place and cause strange things to happen while he was interred there.

The story goes something like this. When, on 16 April, 1117, Earl Hakon murdered his cousin and joint ruler, Earl Magnus, the dead man's mother, Thora, had his body brought from the island of Egilsay where he was slain to be interred in the cathedral of Birsay. About twenty years after he was thus laid to rest, strange happenings took place in Birsay. Around his tomb shone lights while fragrant scents perfumed the air as the blind and the crippled visited Magnus' grave. It is said that some of the maimed who kept vigil there left 'walking straight' or with their eyesight partially restored.

Bishop William, not wishing to displease Earl Hakon and trying to keep in favour with Hakon's son and heir, Earl Paul, refused for many years to give credence to the tales of lights, scents and miraculous cures. However, the political scene was to change radically and, with it, the bishop's mind.

According to the historian, John Mooney, on the day of St Lucy, 13 December, 1135, a great assembly of Orkney's aristocracy, men of letters and learning, assembled in Christ's Kirk by invitation of Bishop William. Before this august gathering he performed the ritual required before bestowing sainthood. The grave of Magnus was opened, the coffin raised and the remains revealed. Then the bones were carefully washed and one bone was selected and three times placed in 'hallowed fire'. It passed the test for it did not burn but took on the appearance of silver cleansed by the flames. All the bones were then placed in a shrine set over the altar and Bishop William proclaimed Magnus to be a saint.

Early in 1136 a solemn procession of clergy and important personages of the earldom made its way from Birsay to Kirkwall bearing the shrine of St Magnus to the church of St Olaf there. We may be sure Earl Paul, son of Hakon, did not take part in this ceremony, for, at the mention of Magnus being a saint, he turned as 'red as blood' with displeasure.

Robert had so timed our visit that the sea was still in retreat when we came to retrace our steps to the Birsay shore. He told me that he'd long had a notion to go on the Brough and stay, marooned there, over a tide. That would have meant a compulsory stay of six hours. I wonder if he ever did it.

As we strolled along, we came to a 'planticru' – a small, walled in cabbage patch – beside the shore. There Robert stopped and in a monotonous, droning voice, very different from his usual high-pitched staccato bursts of speech, recited for me:

The Planticru

Whaur green abune the banks the links stretch oot
On tae the sandy noust, lies midway there
An aald-time planticru, smothered aboot
In weeds – but fu' well delled, and dressed wi' ware,
Biggid o' sea-worn boolders fae the beach
A dyke runs roond it, lichened doun the sides,
Scarce keepan leaf and root beyond the reach
O' winter gales and fierce Atlantic tides.

'Oors lang, an age-bent wife wi' aspect mild
Stands gazan oot tae sea; or digs a speel,
And sets her twa'three tatties i' the dreel;
Nor kens hoo firm she haads b'siklike toil
Man's aald inheritance o' sea and soil.

ROBERT RENDALL

Was this the poem's baptism? Was I the first to hear it? Perhaps not – but I'd like to think so. I still remember the thrill I felt when I first saw it in print in 1951 and recalled that summer evening.

On we walked together and were soon beside the ruins of Robert Stewart's palace. Birsay's village, clustering in its shadow, is called 'The Palace' and I've since read that whoever wrote Robert Stewart's Latin inscription for him over the outer gateway was dangerously inaccurate.

It should have said 'Lord Robert Stewart, son of James the Fifth, King of Scots, erected this building'. What appeared was 'Lord Robert Stewart, King of the Scots, son of James the Fifth, erected this building'. Ironically, Robert Stewart was eventually charged with, among other things, treason, but not as a result of the bad Latin.

However, he did regard himself highly. In November 1567, he described himself as 'feuar of the lands and lordship of Orkney and Zetland and sherriff principal of the samyn'. He then proceeded to make his claim of lordship stick by persuading Bishop Adam Bothwell to hand over to him all the possessions of the bishopric in both island groups in exchange for Holyrood Abbey. His allegedly cruel, tyrannical rule was interrupted by two years in prison, after which he arrived back in Orkney in 1581 to again take up his earldom and, in addition, the title of 'Earl of Orkney'.

None of this tyrant's alleged atrocities were known to me at the time of my Birsay holiday, but as with Noltland Castle in Westray, the gaunt, dark, brooding ruins of the Earl's Palace in Birsay made me shiver uneasily, and I hurried past it when the time came to return to our cosy caravan in the shadowy twilight.

We lived in the caravan, but had our meals at the Beachview Tearoom where delicious home-baked cakes and scones were provided. The tearoom itself was situated within a dark-green wooden building at the edge of Birsay links. It was run by Mrs Flett, whose family lived in the many other rooms of the house. Usually, every rectangular table in that large, white, airy space was occupied by folk unable to resist Mrs Flett's splendid afternoon teas, but at all other times, we were privileged to have it all to ourselves. I contacted Orkney Tourist Information to find out if the Beachview Tearoom still existed, only to discover that the building, now enclosed in bricks, is now a private house.

Eating out was my father's idea, born out of consideration for my mother. He said he wanted her to have a holiday 'not just a change of sink and stove'. Birsay holidays consisted of playing on the beach, clifftop walks and meanders along roads edged with flower-filled ditches. They were happy, carefree days.

One day, however, the world and its troubles interrupted my

happiness. High on bleak Marwick Head towers the lonely memorial to Lord Kitchener, whose face appeared on First World War posters all over the country urging men to go and take part in the slaughter of the trenches. I remember the first time we climbed that imposing hill and my father telling me the words on the well-known 'Your Country Needs YOU' poster. He then went on to recount how, on 5 June, 1916, Lord Kitchener boarded HMS *Hampshire* to go to Russia. Apparently, the ship intended to proceed eastward by Orkney but, as the west side was more sheltered that day, the route was suddenly changed. However, the wind swung round and so whipped up the Atlantic that a destroyer escorting the *Hampshire* was called back to the safety of Scapa Flow. 'How strange,' said my father, 'that no similar signal was sent to the *Hampshire!*' She plunged on until just off Marwick Head where it is thought she struck a mine and sank with nearly all hands.

He went on to tell me that only a few of the crew reached the shore. and were saved. Others, who had attempted to land their raft beneath the high, rugged cliffs, were either killed by being thrown against the rocks or died of exposure. My father ended his story in a way which clearly distressed him. He had been told by local people that when they had eventually been informed of the disaster and wanted to go down the cliffs, by paths only known to them, to rescue any survivors, the military authorities would not allow them to do so.

nine

I was fortunate in our large, multi-denominational household by the side of Kirkwall Bay. Not only was my parents' Brethren influence diluted by my Salvationist grandparents, but also by the Church of Scotland allegiances of my two great-uncles (brothers of my grandmother) and, in early days of the ruling matriarch of our tribe, my great-grandmother, whom I knew as 'Nanny'. There was little fear of my thinking there was only one right religious sect. All those people whom I loved held similar beliefs, but supported different organisations.

Nanny and her husband had had a family pew in the Paterson Church, Kirkwall. It was right in the front of the gallery on the right-hand side of the pulpit. On occasion I sat there beside my Great-uncle Richie but my grandmother took me to the meetings in the Salvation Army Hall.

As I mentioned at the beginning of my story, the Salvation Army Hall was a place of warmth, happiness and fun for me. Many a time it also became a place of great beauty, like when it was decorated for Harvest Festival. Golden sheaves of corn and the fruits of field and garden adorned the hall, making my child's eyes blink in the intensity of colours – purple swedes, dark-red beetroot, fawny onions, deep-orange carrots, golden pears, rosy apples, and bunches of green and black grapes all combined to waft scents of freshly watered, sun-blessed earthiness throughout the building. How heartily we sang:

> Bringing in the sheaves
> Bringing in the sheaves
> We shall come rejoicing
> Bringing in the sheaves.

At a morning service in the Paterson Church, when summer sun streamed and rainbowed through stained glass, my six-year-old eyes used to gaze down with pleasure tinged with envy from my family's pew at the Sunday School pupils. How I longed to be one of them as they swung ankle-socked legs and nodded straw-hatted heads in the front pews beneath, each child bearing an armful of summer flowers. At a certain point in the service, each one went forward to the minister to present his or her sheaf of blooms and these gifts were heaped on the communion table till they became a huge colourful bank of fragrance. Having been blessed, the flowers were distributed to the old, the ill and the lonely. This was known as the Flower Service.

In the Temperance Hall, on a starlit, winter's night those same children had the fun of dressing up in lovely costumes of fairyland and acting in a play. The house lights dimmed, the audience's murmurs ceased and the heavy, dark-red curtains slowly, breath-takingly drew back to reveal a world of fantasy and delight, colour and music. A little boy dressed as an admiral of the fleet with the cocked hat of past years brought the house down with a song, the refrain of which was 'So I'll paddle my own canoe'. How I loved it and how I so intensely ached to be one of those fairies.

No such occurrences brought pleasure to Brethren children. Not even when the Christmas Conference took place on Christmas Day itself. My parents spent the whole afternoon and evening at this gathering, an arrangement which I greatly resented for I felt that this special day of the year would have been even nicer had they been with the rest of the family to enjoy all the Christmassy, after-stocking-opening activities.

No doubt I'll be accused of a lack of spirituality, if not worse, when I say that I did not appreciate the one occasion when I was persuaded to accompany them. No nod was given to the fact it was Christmas. No flower or any form of decoration cheered up the bare meeting house. Not a carol was sung. One fellow regaled us with terrible confessions of the pre-converted, heinous sin of having joined the Boy Scouts. Brethren from rural areas swelled the throng and the lusty volume of the hymn singing.

The Brethren believe their assemblies are modelled on the first churches founded by the Apostle Paul, and aim not to have anything in their meeting place that would distract them from pure worship.

What a good job I did not attend the conference where one earnest preacher ended his homily with the warning 'Johnny, mind your step' but forgot that the platform was raised above the floor, and stepped off into the air to fall flat on his face. Seemingly one old lady cried out in sympathy, but many of the congregation had trouble keeping suitably straight countenances. I believe even a titter or two was to be heard!

The children of the Paterson Church always brought Nanny a bunch of flowers from the Flower Service. She was also visited by the minister. Imagine her Victorian horror when I, sitting as usual on a footstool beside her, emerged from my accustomed silence on such occasions and set about entertaining the stern, prim bachelor, the Reverend Mr Gray, by displaying for him, one by one and slowly, the underclothes given to me with which to dress a doll. I can remember my silent little audience staring speechless at a pair of green, silk bloomers.

My paternal grandmother in Aberdeenshire had taken pity on an unwanted illegitimate child and given her a home. She was my pale-faced Auntie Meg who nursed in a sanatorium for tubercular patients until she contracted the disease herself and died while still quite young. She was a dear, gentle young woman and I loved when she came to us for holidays. She sent me lovely, sweet-faced, china-headed girl dolls with thick, beautifully arranged hair. With each doll came a box of pretty clothes she'd made for it – a red velvet cloak and hood; a sparkling dress of silver lamé; a complete bridal outfit of white silk dress and gossamer veil. Once she proudly told my father that some of her patients had made a selection of the very pretty knitted garments she'd sent me. Immediately, she realised her mistake and hastened to assure him that they'd all been sterilised before being sent to me.

My father had a great fear that I should contract tuberculosis; it was almost a paranoia of his and led him to forbid me to play with a little boy who'd had a gland lanced and so wore a bandage round his neck. I remember when a walk took us past a sanatorium at Scapa and he met an acquaintance who was a patient. On approaching the poor fellow my father quietly but firmly ordered my mother and me to walk on while he stopped to speak to him. When he rejoined us my father remarked that really it would have been safe enough for us to stop as his acquaintance had a metal ball – I think, lead – in his mouth and so would not have passed on the infection. As usual, I never questioned my father, but now I do wish I had asked him more about this unique method of preventing contamination.

Nanny objected vociferously to being left alone at any time. My grandmother and mother used to carry her in her horse-hair armchair from room to room as they did their housework. She was in her nineties and a fall from a stool, which she'd mounted to dust some place out of her reach, had left her crippled and only able to walk with difficulty.

My mother commented to me how strange it was that Nanny and her two sisters, Mary and Sarah, were all lame. They had been crippled as a result of being kicked by cows on their home on the island of North Ronaldsay. It is the most northerly island of Orkney and, like many of the others, it is a low, flat island that, in the days before lighthouses and radar equipment, was often a danger to shipping, hidden, as it frequently was, by blown spray or fog.

My great-grandmother always maintained that her mother arrived on North Ronaldsay because the ship in which she was travelling was one of the many shipwrecked on the island. She did not choose to leave the island, but married and settled there. That must have been in the 1800s.

When my great-grandmother was three years old, in 1841, there were two weavers, one tailor and several joiners, blacksmiths, millers, carpenters and boat-builders on the island. Some of these jobs were done only part-time – farming and fishing being the way most folk made or supplemented their living.

There were no shops, no inns and no shoe-maker. The latter would not have been greatly missed, for my mother recalled that when she visited her great-grandparents one of the first things she did was to exchange her Kirkwall boots for North Ronaldsay footwear. This took the form of a pair of 'rivlins' – slip-on slippers made of rabbit skins; the sole and outer side being skin, and the interior soft, warm rabbit fur.

When my great-grandmother was sixteen, in 1854, the present lighthouse was first lit. It is the highest lighthouse on mainland Britain, though there are taller towers on rocks offshore. My father once told me that the number of steps in North Ronaldsay Lighthouse is the same as the number of verses in the 119th psalm – 176 verses, 176 steps.

Very likely my great-grandmother was away from home by the time the lighthouse flashed in the night sky above the low, flat island. She had moved to Edinburgh where she worked as a cook in the mansion-like Trinity House. I don't know when she met my great-grandfather, who belonged to the Orkney island of Stronsay, but by and by she returned to the Orkney mainland, got married, and brought her three children into the world who, with great delight, sailed to North Ronaldsay each summer to holiday at their grandparents' house.

I expect theirs was like most of the island's thatched cottages – with a 'but' for living in, and a 'ben' which doubled as a room for special occasions as well as being a bedroom. Little closet rooms opened off both main rooms to provide added sleeping accommodation. Joined to the main living area, with a communicating door between, was the steading for the animals and their foodstuffs. Built-in beds, with doors to pull closed, were in every room, and my grandmother recalled lying happily in her box bed, surely unshuttered, watching the flash of the lighthouse illuminate the little window. Although she used the common name, my grandmother was not strictly accurate in her terminology. Box beds – literally, beds enclosed in boxes – stood independently and were often used as partitions, dividing up rooms instead of walls. My grandmother's bed would, more likely, have been one built into a recess in a wall. Both box beds proper and built-in beds had, on their exposed side, wooden shutters or curtains which allowed entry to the bed but which could be closed completely to conceal the occupant. Mattresses in such beds were usually stuffed with chaff from the threshed corn.

When the children returned to Kirkwall, they went sad but not empty-handed. Bottles of home-brewed ale had been prepared and were sent with them to give to Richie, the eldest child, who was considered 'delicate'. The ale was the result of two lengthy processes – the making of the malt, with the addition of hops at one part of the process and their removal at another. Although I have never actually seen North Ronaldsay ale being made, its preparation, which took weeks, is familiar to locals. The corn had to be soaked in water, drained, and then left to germinate. The it was dried further in a kiln before being ground in a stone quern (this was later done in a mill). The resulting malt was then ready to be poured into barrels with hot water and left to infuse after which hops were added. The mixture was then brought to the boil. When it had cooled to blood heat some brewer's yeast was mixed in to cause fermentation. The whole process ended with the ale being strained and bottled. A heated dose of this carefully prepared brew was the tonic administered to strengthen my Great-uncle Richie. I've tasted its modern version, which is made much less laboriously in pristine plastic dustbins, but I pity my great-uncle having to drink it for his health if it tasted at all like its up-to-date counterpart. That said, Great-uncle Richie did live till he was ninety.

Another gift sent to Kirkwall was a container of raw wool from which my Nanny would clean, card, spin and knit clothes for the family. Her father had his share of sheep, each one bearing on its ears its owner's particular cut-out mark to distinguish it from the animals belonging to other islanders. Those marks were essential, for the goat-like sheep were not enclosed in the fields of a farm, but, as they still do, roamed the beach, kept off the island's pastures and cultivated areas by a stone wall about six feet high that encircled the island. Their grazing was the red seaweeds cast ashore by the storms or left exposed each time the sea ebbed.

So when the little Kirkwallians holidayed in North Ronaldsay, they probably had mutton to eat as well as 'cuithes' fresh from the sea, followed by oatcakes or bere bannock both made from home-grown crops of small, black oats and bere corn respectively. And from all those kicking cows that crippled my great-great aunts there would have been butter and cheese to eat, and milk, supplemented by ale, to drink, as well as fresh, sweet water carried home from the well.

When my grandmother, the only girl of the family, had her own two daughters, she took them in their turn to the family home in North Ronaldsay. My mother remembered, besides the 'rivlins' for her feet, the carvy plants in the garden from which dark, bitter seeds were plucked to be baked in carvy biscuits. She recalled, too, how the cow pats had to be collected and dried to provide fuel for the fire. Tangles from the beach and cast-up pieces of wood which could not be used for anything else were also dried and burned. North Ronaldsay has no indigenous fuel. Before the importing of coal, the islanders had to sail over to the island of Eday where they cut and prepared peat which they boated home for their fires.

Imagine the stories told to those generations of children as they sat by the open hearth in their straw-backed stools – now called 'Orkney chairs' – in a room of shadows. Perhaps they heard how the 'selchies', the local name for seals, cast off their skins and in human form danced on the sand or ventured inland and married ordinary mortals, usually with disastrous results. As the 'cruisie' lamp burned – a pan with a wick soaked in the oil from fish livers or seal fat – perhaps the children heard of the fairies on the island who would on occasion help people in return for gifts of food. Huddled together, young minds would have soaked up tales of those malignant fairies who put spells on folk or kidnapped them, taking them away never to be seen again or to be replaced by some unpleasant being. These fairies lived underground in mounds.

I wonder what would be found if some of these mounds were excavated. Bronze Age stone burial cists have been found in North Ronaldsay. One mound had been hiding a group of dwelling places with a scattering of the inhabitants' domestic utensils still extant. There were sheep- and whale-bone implements such as combs, pot-lids, weaving equipment, a stone quern for grinding corn and crudely made pottery. Archaeologists believe these things belonged to people of the Bronze or Iron Age. A broch, one of those circular stone towers which are thought to have been places of refuge when enemies approached, was examined in North Ronaldsay and besides whale-bone articles there were objects made of bronze, iron and deerhorn. More surprising, there were objects with Pictish symbols on them and a bell from a Celtic church.

In my husband's native parish of Deerness on Orkney's mainland there is a mound which was believed to be a home of the fairies, and we have been told that it is most likely to have been a broch.

Did the people who hid in brochs when alien ships landed continue to live underground as the invaders settled? Did they perhaps only come up for fresh air and necessities in the hours of darkness and thus give rise to the belief that they were supernatural beings? I'm only speculating but the oral superstition surrounding such places was very real and written history, too, tells tales of strange happenings in North Ronaldsay. In the *Orkneyinga Saga* the island is, of course, called by its Norse name, *Rinansey*. The first recorded incident on the island under Norse rule is horrific. It was there that the earl Turf Einar sacrificed the King of Norway's son, Halfdan Halegg, to the god Odin. His ribs were severed and his lungs pulled out thus carving a blood eagle on his back and making him an acceptable sacrifice to the god of war. The king's son was buried and a cairn raised over him, perhaps to become another of the mysterious mounds.

ten

My great-grandparents first lived as close to the sea as possible in a house in Shore Street, Kirkwall, commonly called 'The Shore'. Perhaps they felt that by living there they were as near their island homes as they could be; perhaps the sea provided a visible link to their past. It must have been a traumatic change to come from the beauty and freedom of their islands to the enclosed, circumscribed life of a town – a little grey town by the sea clustered round its pink sandstone cathedral.

I can't say as much about my great-grand-father's island of Stronsay as I have about North Ronaldsay, home of my great-grandmother. Having only walked through the attractive village of Whitehall while the north isle boat on which I was travelling unloaded supplies at Stronsay pier, I haven't seen the sandy beaches, the crumbling cliffs with ledges upholstered by the feathered bodies of sea-birds and the masses of wild flowers that carpet the wasteland. I haven't been in North Ronaldsay at all, but my folk spoke more about it.

In 1670, Patrick Fea, who at one time made his fortune by privateering on the high seas, bought land in Stronsay which included the place now occupied by the village. Where the head of the pier now is, he built a house called 'Whitehall', and its name came to be applied to his entire property.

Patrick's son, James Fea, started the kelp industry in Orkney in 1722. Kelp was made by collecting, drying, and reducing to ashes, rock weeds, and later the seaweed called 'tangles'. The ashes were exported to be used in the manufacture of glass, soap and iodine. This industry continued until the nineteenth century and was so attractive a source of money for landlords and working folk alike that agricultural work was often neglected while people laboured to make the more lucrative kelp.

According to the 1793 First Statistical Account for Kirkwall and St Ola, kelp-making was not initially welcomed in Orkney. It was feared it would ruin the fishing by driving the fish from the coast; it would destroy the crops and grass; it would make the women sterile. However, when the power of money began to be felt in a place where it had been rarely acquired and then only in pittances, people accepted the new industry with enthusiasm. During times of crop failure when near-famine conditions prevailed, as they did around 1780, where previously people had faced starvation, now they were able to buy food. The poor were better fed, housed and clothed, thanks to the kelp.

However, there is another side to the picture. Not only was agriculture neglected, but food prices rose along with income and landlords adopted a style of living which their estates alone could not support. The writer of the 1793 Statistical Account warns that should the kelp industry fall on bad days, ruin would be the lot of landlord and tenant alike.

As it turned out, however, during the nineteenth century and up to the period between the two wars, Stronsay enjoyed a boom in the herring fishing. Fishing stations came into being on Stronsay itself and its satellite island, Papa Stronsay. I remember fisher-girls from North-east Scotland, returning from the Stronsay fishing, lying helplessly sea-sick on the deck of the north-isle boat. My father, who'd been brought up in Aberdeenshire and knew the fishing communities of the coastal towns and villages, used to be so angry at how poorly the girls were housed and cared for when they came to work in Orkney. He used to exclaim angrily, 'If they could see the homes those folk come from – you could eat your dinner off their doorsteps.'

The time of prosperous fishing – when the population of Stronsay rose from a few hundred to over 6,000 in the summer, and when shops and businesses were starting to meet the needs of so many more people – came to an end when the Second World War broke out.

My great-grandfather would have been away from Stronsay before the time of prosperity. He'd have known it as a quiet island of farming, fishing and kelp-making. My mother thought he was a farmer before coming to Kirkwall where he got a job at the pier. After a fall, he was put in charge of the animals that came from the islands, and which had to be kept in the town until the boats sailing south could ship them to the Scottish mainland.

During the time my great-grandfather was so employed, there came to Orkney an enterprising young man called Robert Garden. He began to make his living by selling things from a barrow and ended up ruling a little commercial empire. He had a large shop selling drapery, china and ironmongery. To back this there was a wholesale warehouse. He owned a grinding mill; he had a grocer's shop; he sold seeds and manure; and he even fitted out sailing smacks as shops to take his trade to the islands and along the north coast of Scotland.

My great-uncle was employed by him as a baker. My grandmother worked in the drapery and also in the dressmaking and millinery departments. In their turn, my mother and aunt had jobs in the drapery shop. My father, who came to Orkney after the first war, was one of Garden's drapers and so met my mother. Eventually he became manager of the drapery shop.

Robert Garden owned two streets – Garden Street and Garden's Buildings where he housed his employees and his relatives. In Garden's Buildings my great-grandparents, with my Great-uncle Richie and my aunt, had a downstairs flat while my grandparents and my parents lived in an upstairs flat next door.

I was born in this upstairs flat and, after only three weeks of life, nearly died there. Children, eager to see the new baby, but still only recovering from whooping cough, passed on the virus to me. The old midwife who cared for my mother told my parents on one occasion that it was no use troubling the doctor any more for I was dead. My father, however, did run to fetch Dr Sinclair who, as my mother put it, 'breathed his breath into me' by putting his mouth covered with a handkerchief on mine, and I revived. Dr Sinclair surely knew about mouth-to-mouth resuscitation more than half a century ago.

So, thanks to Dr Sinclair whom I regarded in terror in later years, so brusque was his manner, I lived to shovel snow and 'help' my father make a snow house for me when the cold, white wreaths lay higher than my head in 'the back', as the sort of courtyard behind Garden's Buildings was called. Icicles, like translucent swords, fringed the eaves of outside wash-houses and water closets. I was alive to laugh and weep. One sunny day I recall doing both. I had lined my dolls against our back wall only to have two of them stolen by a neighbouring rascal. In silent, dismayed and uncomprehending amazement I watched her march off with them, before rushing home in floods of tears. When she had calmed me, my gallant little grandmother made a foray to the offender's home and retrieved the treasures so precious to my two-year-old's heart. I lived to enjoy days when the rain dropped like tears on the window pane and I swung on a swing erected indoors for me. Surely it swung above the table for I remember my silver-haired Great-uncle Richie looking up at me as he ate his meal.

My great-grandmother must have become very attached to her dwelling in Garden's Buildings for, when my grandfather built 'The Moorings' out Cromwell's Road for the entire family, only a few hundred yards distant, she could only be persuaded to go to live there by the need to accompany me to the new house. I remember our slow progress there – Nanny, dressed all in black, her skirt reaching to the ground and an elaborately swathed silk hat on her head, tapping along with her walking stick, and I, aged three, my hand in hers, trotting beside her extolling the virtues of our new home by Kirkwall Bay – no doubt repeating propaganda fed me to win her over to the same side as the rest of the family.

Anyhow she eventually settled in, enclosed by coldly distempered walls and ever-open, shiningly clean windows for my Great-uncle

Richie believed papered walls bred disease and a constant stream of fresh air was necessary to keep people healthy. 'Open that window,' was his immediate cry if anybody closed one in protest against the indoor gale. 'See that all the windows are shut,' came the order when he appeared with his window-cleaning equipment which consisted of a giant syringe-like implement by which he hosed down each pane with forceful jets of water drawn up from a zinc bucket. This over, he lost no time in countermanding his initial instruction with 'Open all windows'.

On Sunday nights, when every member of the household felt called to his or her place of worship, there was a rota of what would now be described as 'baby sitters' or – more accurately in our case – 'baby and great-grandmother sitters'. One Sabbath evening it was my father's turn to sit with Nanny and me. On Nanny's wall hung a gloomy black-and-white picture of a shepherd reaching over a precipice to rescue a lamb. I, silly fool, asked about this scene. My father, a Victorian sentimentalist if ever there was one, told me in a tremulous voice, and piling on pathos, the story of the little lost lamb. He hadn't bargained for the result – heart-breaking sobs and pools of tears which would not be assuaged no matter how hard he tried to reach a happy ending. He stood no chance of drawing human parallels or pointing out morals – my grief for the vicissitudes the poor little lamb had experienced knew no bounds and I refused to hear another word.

Nanny, a helpless onlooker, at length urged me to accept a pandrop. It wasn't a wise move either for the next thing they knew they had a purple-faced, choking child to bang on the back.

My father either didn't understand what had caused the uproar or else refused to learn from experience what kind of stories to avoid in front of me. I took to excusing myself from the table and running outside the back door where I'd stand with my hands over my ears till I thought he'd finished some of his more heart-wringing tales with which he entertained guests. He did not approve of my unappreciative behaviour.

The story I think I detested most of all was about a shepherd boy called Roderick who lived in the Highlands A minister taught this child to say 'The Lord is My Shepherd' touching each finger of one hand in turn with the index finger of the other as he said every word. By and by there came the inevitable snowstorm and, to cut a long story short, when Roderick's corpse was found, the index finger of one hand was stuck to the fourth finger of the other, thus demonstrating how he had spent his last living moments. Harrowing stuff!

My mother knew me better or accepted my sensibilities as they were. She found that the usual, published stories for children were too strong meat for me at bedtime. No, what I wanted to hear was of a 'peedie' girl who went walking one day and who should she meet but a pussy-cat who led her to a family of kittens. On another occasion this same peedie girl met a dog who took her to a litter of puppies. An understanding, jolly farmer's wife was usually involved in the happy ending when the child returned home with kitten or puppy, depending on which animals were favoured that evening. I had Poma, my dearly-loved, grey-and-white cat from Eday and looked upon Great-uncle Richie's black-and-white collie dog, Mac, as my dog. So there was no difficulty in identifying with the equally cat and dog blessed heroine.

When I began to teach, I asked my mother where she'd found those delightful tales. 'Oh I just made them up as anything else only upset you,' was her reply.

So *Chicks' Own* was the only mild enough comic, and *Sunny Stories* and *Fairyland Tales,* two little magazines containing stories, that I knew would not play on my emotions and make me miserable. *Chicks' Own's* cheerfully coloured front page was taken up with the gentle adventuring of a yellow chick and a black chick, and nothing more alarming appeared within. I think *Sunny Stories* and *Fairyland Tales* – again with bright, cheerful covers – were the delightful outpourings of Enid Blyton. Children have always loved her stories and still do. In my little tuppenny magazines I discovered the adventures of The Wishing Chair, which stood in the nursery and grew wings and took the children on happy journeys; there were visits to The Faraway Tree where you had to watch out for Dame Washalot's washing water and listen for the clanking of the Saucepan Man; and in the toy cupboard lived Amelia Jane, the big, naughty doll, who displayed such bad behaviour that I gasped at her daring and felt deliciously virtuous.

Victoria Hall Sunday School usually presented me with the highly moral tales of Amy Le Feuvre as prizes for perfect attendance. I hardly deserved the honour as I had no option but to be at Sunday School each and every week. *Teddy's Button* and *The Cherry Tree* were two of the titles. I remember how Teddy had to decide between staying with his poor, but noble-minded, highly moral family or moving into the country mansion of his well-off uncle and aunt, who, being childless, wished to adopt Teddy and tempted him with a pony and other gains to be had by choosing a life of luxury with them. In the end, Teddy turned his back on wealth, deciding not to become a 'money-grubber'.

Amy Le Feuvre's books were more bearable than the old prize books of my grandmother, mother and aunt in which good little Victorians or their saintly mothers were forever being transported prematurely to Heaven. Many a bitter tear I shed over such demises and, because of those fictitious deaths, on top of the Brethren's teachings, I lived in almost constant fear and anxiety of similar removals taking place in our house.

Not surprisingly, the stories I made up while pushing my doll's pram round our garden on the neat, concrete paths were always pleasant. But they were more than stories – they were adventures in an imaginary world; the world of an island which I situated, but hidden, among the beautiful island panorama to be seen from 'The Moorings'. It was called 'Fare-thee-well Island' and one of the population, who was my special friend, was a girl called Jeannie. The sunny, yellow and orange marigolds; the high, sky-blue delphiniums; the deep-red roses; the nodding pink and blue lupins; and the sweet-scented honeysuckle were my audience for the news from 'Fare-thee-well'. So engrossed did I become in my one-sided conversations that I wasn't at all aware of the butcher boy's puzzled stares until one day, having observed me for some time, he asked my mother with concern – 'Is the peedie lass right in the heid? She's speakin' tae the flooers.'

I also found an audience in the child dummies for displaying clothes that stood about in what I called 'Daddy's shop'. Sometimes, though, when I touched their cold, plaster fingers, I did rather wish they could say something back to me.

The shop where my father worked was a sort of treasure cave for me.

I especially liked the china department with its crystal objects a-sparkle and a-glitter in their lit-up, velvet-lined niches. With what dismay, indeed horror, did I wake up one night to find everybody dashing about in alarm. Garden's was on fire!

My father's greatest concern was that the conflagration be brought under control before it reached the huge oil tanks in which the whole of Orkney's supplies were stored. He always had thought it foolish to build those tanks right behind the shop and amongst people's dwellings. 'One spark and the whole thing will blow up!' he announced dramatically. I believe that at least the house nearest the tanks was evacuated while the fire raged, so more than he feared an explosion.

My concern was for his job, but soon I had it worked out for him. 'Betty's Daddy' – he was Garden's head baker – 'will bake pies, and you will go round the town selling them.' My father greeted this plan for a future career with a silent smile.

The shop was almost totally destroyed. Of the beautiful china department some pyrex dishes, standing up to surely their greatest test of heat endurance, were found completely intact. However, the wholesale warehouse and drapery store were untouched and so my father's position as manager was preserved. Thankfully, my suggestion that he venture into the pie-selling business was not required.

In the wholesale department was a goods lift that rumbled up and down when my father or his young assistant hauled on thick, heavy ropes. From a safe distance I enjoyed watching mysterious straw hampers, wooden or cardboard boxes and brown paper parcels of all shapes and sizes appear as if by magic at floor level from some unknown, unimaginable underground treasure trove.

From a safe distance, too, I watched the local tinkers fill their huge cloth packs which they carried round the countryside on their backs, selling the bed-linen, towels and other drapery which they bought from my father, conversing with him as they did so in their peculiar clipped accents. Old Robbie, one might say, had a real way with words. One day, speaking to my father about the First World War, he asked, 'Did you hear aboot the day that a German Soup Tureen sank a British destroyer in Scapa Flow?' Up to date with the 1939–45 conflict he remarked:

'Hitler is a bad lot, but nothing like Mrs Mussolini. I canna put up wi' her. Ye never ken whit she'll dae next.'

Then, before Christmas, part of the wholesale warehouse was divided off and turned into a toy-shop. The shelves were crammed to capacity with wonderful toys that all together composed a kaleidoscope of colour and excitement. There were dolls dressed in rich velvets, jewel-bright satins and pretty, cool cottons. There were gaily coloured wooden hoops with handles and little silver bells that tinkled as you pushed the hoop along. Clockwork toys painted brightly in every colour of the rainbow were wound up and performed in all sorts of delightful and novel ways. Boxes of games packaged in gay, attractively coloured boxes were ranged round the room. It was a display of dreams. Children of the staff were allowed to choose a toy which Santa would present at a Christmas party. Only the terrible longing for a dark-eyed doll with long, thick, golden plaits made me endure that noisy party, and pluck up enough courage to approach the bewhiskered gentleman in red to obtain it. I never in childhood got over this fear of Santa Claus. When much older, at a Brownie party, I begged and begged a Guide helper to go to the mythical figure on my behalf.

In fact, I was an ultra nervous party-goer. Even the sedate parties held in the sitting-rooms of my friends' homes were something of a strain. From the time the white-capped and aproned maid helped me change from my black, shiny shoes into black dancing pumps, smoothed down the pale-green silk petals that composed the skirt of my party dress, adjusted the little circular 'pocket' for my handkerchief that hung by a cord round my neck and had been crocheted by my aunt to match my dress, till the last tinkling notes on the piano brought the final 'Farmer's in his den', 'Ring o' Roses', or 'Nuts in May' to an end, I was not entirely at ease.

Some games we seemed to play only at parties. There was 'Here's the robbers passing by' played as elsewhere is played 'Oranges and Lemons.' Our words were more sinister. 'What's the robbers done to you, My fair lady?' we asked in the second verse, to which the reply came:

Broke my locks and stole my gold.
Into prison they must go
They must go, they must go
Into prison they must go
My fair lady.

Then as each child in the wending column passed beneath the arch made by two members, the following words were uttered 'Breakfast, Dinner, Tea, Supper – Grupper'. On this last word the arch came down and made prisoner the person passing through at that moment. The prisoner then chose in secret an orange or a lemon and so decided on which side of the arch to stand and support in the final tug of war.

'Here we come gathering nuts in May,' also ended in tugs of war, but only between two people at a time.

Here we come gathering nuts in May
Nuts in May, Nuts in May,
Here we come gathering Nuts in May
On a cold and frosty morning.

One line of children advanced hand in hand towards an opposing line and retreated, advanced and retreated throughout the verse.

'Who do you want for "Nuts in May"?' enquired the other line repeating the performance.

'We'll have Margaret Donald for "Nuts in May",' and my heart fluttered – pleased to have been chosen but embarrassed at being singled out for attention.

Who will you choose to pull her away,
Pull her away, pull her away
Who will you choose to pull her away
On a cold and frosty morning.

Our opponents held a whispered consultation, and then after much deliberation announced that: 'We'll send Janet Sutherland to pull her away.' Janet and I would then advance to the centre between the two lines and try each to pull the other to her own side.

Even to our innocent hearts there was no point in playing a game without boys which went:

In and out the windows
In and out the windows
In and out the windows
As we have gone before.

Stand and face your lover
Stand and face your lover
Stand and face your lover
As we have done before.

Follow him to London
Follow him to London
Follow him to London
As we have done before.

'And it was sunk by a German submarine,' we joyfully carolled in a circle joined by crossed arms at the end of the 'Alley, alley o'.

A big ship sails through the Alley, Alley o,
The Alley, Alley o
The Alley, Alley o
A big ship sails through the Alley, Alley o
On the fourteenth of September.

The ship's progress was conveyed by a long line passing under an arch made by the head of the line placing her hand on the wall. As the attached line wound right through, the first person was turned round and her arms crossed. Then the line passed under the next arch made by the joined hands of the first and second person who at the end of the procession was turned round and arms crossed.

However, we did not confine singing games to parties. In the playground or on the almost vehicle-free roads we'd circle round a kneeling figure singing mournfully:

> Here's a little sandy girl
> Sitting all alone
> Crying, weeping all the day long
> Rise up, sandy girl
> Wipe your tears away
> Choose the one you love the best
> And run, run away.

Two older cousins and their friends included me in a game whose words puzzled me greatly then and still do. This usually took place in a garden which seemed an appropriate setting to me for we were singing about flowers – or were we?

> Wally, wally wallflowers growing up so high
> We are all maidens so we must all die
> Except Pine Foubister for she's the youngest one
> She shall dance and she shall sing
> And she shall wear a wedding ring.
> Fie, fie, fie for shame
> Turn her face to the wall again.

At this point the chosen one had to walk round backwards, still attached to the circle.

To me, these everyday games were much more fun than those played at parties. Indeed, my idea of a really comfortable social occasion was when my Aunt Lilla invited me 'ben the hoose' where she, Nanny and Great-uncle Richie resided, to drink mugs of steaming pinky-brown cocoa with them in front of the fire. Nowhere has cocoa ever tasted so good. It was in their living-room that in later years I browsed through the bookcase and chose book after book. That was when my taste for my cousin Thora's old *Schoolgirl* annuals waned, and I'd done my weeping over Matthew's death in *Anne of Green Gables*.

I once asked a schoolgirl from one of the north isles of Orkney how it had felt to leave home and come to live in one of the school hostels in Kirkwall. 'Great,' she said, 'just like all the schoolgirl stories I'd ever read coming true.' I was glad she enjoyed it for she really did not have much choice in the matter. Like all those who wished to proceed to higher education, she had to board away from her smaller island home while attending the necessary senior secondary classes. One of the many fascinating points that kept me reading avidly the stories of such boarding-school girls was their language. I remember, for example, my amusement at the way Paula, the elegant, appearance- and fashion-conscious dimwit of the 5th Form of St Somebody's, referred to her companions as 'Geals'. Even stranger was the question of how she would have pronounced it.

Great-uncle Richie's bookcase was also full of what were regarded as 'the classics', all bound in red board, their titles lettered in gold. He had collected them through some sort of scheme started by his favourite newspaper, *The Daily Herald*. With readings from this same paper, he used to either bore or entertain my aunt every evening after supper. My aunt never said how she looked upon his news broadcasts and I never could guess as she just listened in silence and went on with her crochet.

I ploughed through Sir Walter Scott's pages and revelled in the *Heart of Midlothian* and *Ivanhoe*. I leapt with Pip on meeting Magwitch in the churchyard, grieved over Estella's and Miss Haversham's cruelty to him, and sorrowed for the poor old convict caught in the end. As for Little Nell and her grandfather – I could not bear it. I smiled through Mr Pickwick's escapades and enjoyed all Jane Austen's novels. My tears fell copiously over *Jane Eyre*, *Wuthering Heights* and *The Mill on the Floss*.

My grandmother thought it quite despicable of females to neglect home duties by reading novels – I can still hear the scorn with which she invested the word 'novels' – but surely she didn't realise that 'Richie's books', as she called them, belonged to that category, for she only rarely said, rather tetchily, when I'd been sitting for hours with my head in a book, 'It's time you were doing something in your hands and no' spendin' so much time on books.'

Even on Sundays, when normal week-day reading was completely forbidden, I used to find in the bottom shelf of the bookcase something that was allowed on the Sabbath. My aunt took *The Sunday Companion* and *The Christian Herald*. Their very titles rendered them safe. Eagerly I waited from one weekend to the next for each episode in the serials.

I was incredibly glad to have something to read for it was always on Sundays that my sister and I seemed to begin a game that turned out to be more exciting than usual and certainly much too wild for the Sabbath day. How often we tried to walk round the kerb which ran along the garden path without slipping off. Sure enough our laughing would attract a face to the window, a sharp rap and a warning call – 'Remember, it's the Sabbath!' End of fun! Sundays in Orkney were pretty dull, at least for us, and it is little wonder that I became so entranced by Great-uncle Richie's bookcase.

eleven

Choosing prize books won at school took me hours. We were taken to Leonards, a local bookshop to make our choices, and of course it took me a great deal of time and effort to make sure the books I chose contained no dark, frightening pictures that could mean dark, frightening stories lurked between their covers.

To begin with I didn't accept my enforced attendance at school at all willingly in fact I dashed off home whenever I could. The trigger for my escape routine was a recurring 'daymare'.

In the Baby Class, as the infant class was called, we sat in small, wooden chairs with curved, barred backs in front of a three-sided rectangular shape made by long, wooden tables. I remember little of the stories as I sat tortured by a dreaded neighbour who passed the time by pulling the short hairs at the back of my neck.

One storytime, however, has a special place in my memory. As we sat round in in our chairs, the teacher told the Bible story of Joseph and his coat of many colours. My gentle-voiced teacher innocently dwelt on the fact that Joseph's brothers had killed a lamb in order to cover the coat with blood when, much to her distress and bewilderment, I burst into tears and would not be comforted. Joseph's predicament was heart-rending enough, but the fate of the lamb distressed me beyond measure. Come to think of it, sheep seem to have played a considerable part in my emotional life. Maybe this has something to do with heredity, for my paternal grandfather and all his sons, with the exception of my father, were shepherds. The only nod I personally made to this family vocation was when I went to a Brownie Fancy Dress Party as Little Bo-peep, my costume copying exactly that portrayed in Nursery Rhyme books. On that occasion I carried a beautifully carved shepherd's crook, which, if I remember correctly, had been given to my father by my shepherd grandfather.

Most afternoons in the Baby Class we lifted our chairs and carried them round to the back of the tables on which we then built blocks or modelled with plasticine. It was then that the 'daymare' occurred. Suddenly, I saw in my mind red flames bursting out all over our house and two completely black figures struggling to get out. I knew those silhouettes were May and Mammy. I simply had to get home at once.

'Please, Miss, may I leave the room?'

'We-ell you're not to run home if I let you.'

'No, Miss.'

'Then all right – but no running home.'

She could have saved her breath. I was through that door like a shot, up the dark, stone-floored corridor, out through the main door, then the school gate, and home as fast as my legs would carry me. Panting, often with a stitch in my side, I hurled myself inside and collapsed on a chair in the dear, familiar kitchen. There they were – my mother and grandmother in their dust-caps and aprons as usual, safe and sound, cleaning our already spotless house.

I don't know how long this carry-on persisted, but my family were at their wits' end as to what to do about it. In the mornings I was sick and May, having warmed my coat and boots at the kitchen fire, as was her wont for all of us, saw me safely into the dreaded edifice. Again at lunch-time, I pleaded to stay at home and my father had to escort me back. He wrung out hanky after hanky at the drinking fountain in the playground as my distressed nose soaked one after the other with blood.

By the fountain were the shelter sheds, which were attached to one wall of the disgusting, smelly lavatories. The shelter sheds, as we called them, were really a sort of roofed lean-to, where we could shelter if the weather turned bad during play-time. Sometimes a teacher would accompany us on our official, time-tabled parades to those awful toilets with their ancient pre-flushing arrangement, but on those other times when we trotted back two by two and hand in hand, we'd form a circle in the draughty shelter sheds and play 'Hullaballoo, balloo', the predecessor of the modern day 'Looby Loo' and 'Hokey, Kokey.'

Hullaballoo, balloo,
Hullaballoo, ballae,
Hullaballoo, balloo
All on a Saturday night.

Put your right hand in
Put your right hand out
Shake it a little a little
And turn yourself about.

Hullaballoo, balloo etc.

There was a jutting out ridge of a cream-coloured stone along the back wall of the shelter where we rubbed our cold, hard, scratchy slate pencils to sharpen them. An old tobacco box of my Great-uncle Richie's held my bit of wet sponge to wash my slate though I seem to remember the teacher sprinkling water on our slates from a bottle. A dry cloth was also carried to dry those purply-blue rectangles in their worn smooth wooden frames.

The little soaking sponge in its soon red-rusted tin; the damp duster; my paper poke with a jammed scone, biscuit and banana, all combined with the leather of my schoolbag, and when I opened my school bag each morning the sight of my lovingly wrapped play-piece, neatly folded duster, box of slate pencils and reading book, all carefully arranged inside, not only overwhelmed me with a most distinctive, indescribable aroma, but with a wave of homesickness. I was filled with a longing to be back with those kind hands that had busied themselves preparing and arranging the contents of my bag.

Happily, a little boy of my age came to stay out our road, and took to calling for me on the way to school and accompanying me home. Everything changed because of this well-mannered, pleasant-natured young gentleman – for a gentleman Alan was. I faced school with a new and satisfactory degree of equanimity from then on.

Some days, Alan and I used to call on my Great-uncle Johnny's wife, Clara, and her mother, Grannie Mowat, and Clara always gave us each a newly baked cake topped with white icing and as light as a feather. Alan's mother used to invite me to play in their house when darkness encroached early into winter days and introduced me to the delight of eating boiled egg mashed up in a cup with bread and butter. The taste, even the thought, of this dish will ever bring me back to those happy days. When the time came to go home, I remember how Alan, ever gallant, used to walk ahead of me to protect me from the hard, sore hailstones that sometimes greeted us on the way.

I don't know why Alan didn't join me on my Wednesday afternoon treats. Wednesday afternoon was my father's half-day holiday and he always, to my great joy, came to meet me coming out of school. Then we'd go along the ice-cream shop, where he'd give me and a boy called Jimmy a ha'penny cornet. Since Jimmy was my classmate, but no special friend, I rather think that he had this end in sight when he accompanied us on our weekly walk!

Sometimes my mother also appeared on a Wednesday carrying a bag, which was an added treat, for it meant we were going on a picnic! We would make our way out of town in a westerly direction along the Ayre Road.

It was from this same road that, when I was three, we one day watched flying boats swooping to land before speeding over the sea to rise again. I am sure of the year for on that same day a little boy from Deerness celebrated his third birthday in town and he and his grandfather had also watched the great, heavy, unwieldy-looking aircraft send up fountains of white, churned up sea. He told me after I'd married him more than twenty years later.

My parents and I walked past the smelly 'Peedie Sea' to grassy banks by the Ayre shore, not far from where the turbulent tides tumbled and tossed under an arched bridge. This arch with its tumult of waters was called 'The Eye' and was 'very dangerous', my parents warned. On grass as soft as carpet we would drink our lemonade and eat our biscuits – nectar from the gods could not have tasted better.

If Wednesday was a day to be looked forward to, Mondays and Thursdays became days to be dreaded. I was enrolled with a spinster lady who would teach me to play the piano. Though I greatly desired to have my fingers grow long and thin, and my mother assured me they would if I became a pianist, and though I listened with pleasure, consumed with a longing to emulate, my aunt and my cousin Thora as they filled the air with recognisable melodies, I hadn't bargained for a long, slow uphill task or the ordeal which my piano lessons turned out to be.

The sofa, on which I sat and endured the stumblings of my unpractised predecessor, watching fearfully the teacher's face turn turkey-cock red with fury, was made of black horsehair and pricked my bare legs. In embarrassment and terror – for I hadn't practised overmuch either – I lifted my eyes to the picture above the piano. It portrayed a scene of battle, probably Waterloo, in which horses rolled whinnying in anguish on the ground and men lay about spattered with blood, while hosts, bearing banners, clashed swords above them. To my left was a highly polished chest of drawers on which stood a glass-fronted box displaying many beautiful doomed butterflies, and wax fruit lay arranged beneath a glass dome.

There were compensations for undergoing this ordeal. My legs felt as light as on the first day I was allowed to change stockings for socks as I skipped home on a Thursday at 6 o'clock. Piano lessons and the angry teacher could be forgotten till next week, and there would be fried tatties for tea. This culinary delight only appeared on Thursdays. Other gastronomic treats on our menu were hot, spicy ginger wine in winter; cool, sparkling, white-frothed Boston Cream on hot summer days; slices of dumpling, filled with fruit and wrapped-up silver thruppenny bits on birthdays; and a soup-plate full of boiled onions prepared for supper by my grandfather if he thought any of us were heading for colds.

It was almost a pleasure to have a cold in our house, though the block of camphor sewn into my liberty bodice was supposed to prevent this happening. Besides the onion supper, my chest was rubbed with warm, camphorated oil. I preferred May to do this and when I told her how nice her fingers felt, she'd demur, 'They're gey coorsh, budda. That's wi' hard work.'

Besides the piano the only other percussion instrument with which I had any truck was the school bell. It hung in the belfry of Kirkwall Grammar School. Posses of little girls clustered round the door of the bell tower, leaping up and down, arms outstretched, hands waving, pleading, 'Me, me, me', when the teacher appeared from inside to choose the lucky pair who'd ring the bell. It was considered a great privilege to pull the bell rope and set the bell clanging over Kirkwall, and exciting games of 'Relieving Picko', 'Stoney Picko' and 'Statues' were happily relinquished to win the honour.

It was a bell rung in St Magnus Cathedral that summoned the scholars of the Grammar School of the eighteenth century. When the pupils, all boys, heard it, they had to hasten back from their playtime activities in the fields of Buttquoy and Brandyquoy or run up School Wynd, now Tankerness Lane, from the shores of the Oyce, now the 'Peedie Sea.' Those places would not have been too distant, for the Grammar School of that time was situated in the vicinity of the present day David Spence's bookshop at the top of Broad Street.

Those boys must have been glad of their breaks, for they started at seven in the morning and worked till six in the evening three days of the week, and till four the two other days. Saturday education only lasted for the morning. They had two playtimes, one from nine to ten and a two hour interval from 12 till 2. Sunday saw them ranged in the Cathedral's School Loft. A few were put through their paces in public by having to recite the Catechism in front of the congregation. After the service, it was back to school to be questioned on the sermon.

It would have been quite common to hear Latin spoken on the streets of Kirkwall, for the Grammar schoolboys were expected to speak it outside school as well as inside. Part of the disciplinary procedure was to have appointed 'Censors' who were to report any pupil heard speaking English, swearing, cursing or lying or caught throwing stones, sailing on the sea or keeping late bed-times. The headmaster himself might call on parents to check that his charges were saying their prayers regularly as directed and behaving in a seemly fashion.

When James III of Scotland in 1486, handed over the Cathedral of St Magnus to the magistrates of Kirkwall, he also put in their keeping the schools and their lands.

At that time there was not only a Grammar School but a Sang School whose teacher had to be qualified to teach music, primarily so that his pupils could sing satisfactorily in the Cathedral. It is thought that an establishment to ensure satisfactory music in the Cathedral would have existed from the time the church began to be used for worship – as early as the twelfth century, Earl Rognvald, the founder's, own period.

Bishop Reid built a college in which to house the Grammar School of the sixteenth century, and it took the successive deaths of three schoolmasters to convince the Burgh Council of 1764 that there was something far wrong with the state of this aged building.

A poor, earthen-floored erection was put up near the Cathedral. It could have been little better than Bishop Reid's old place for the elements met with little opposition and played havoc in it to such an extent that no teacher could be persuaded to work in it. At last, in 1820, the Burgh Council aided by many generous contributors, managed to build a new school.

There were more schools than the Grammar School, and around 1850, three of those were integrated – the Grammar School, the Subscription School and the Infant School, and a new building was put up to house them – the building with our bell tower as a novel and special feature. My grandmother always referred to our school as the 'Burgh School'. I suppose that would have been its name when the integration took place.

In 1873, besides the three now housed as one, there were a Society School, Charity School, General Assembly School and seven private schools, which included a seminary for young ladies.

My afore-mentioned 'delicate' great-uncle would have started his education about 1877. However, because his mother thought he wasn't strong enough to be thrust into the rough and tumble of the Burgh School, she sent him to a private fee-paying establishment presided over by a lady called Miss Goldie. I think she lived in East Road. On reaching the age-limit for Miss Goldie's school he was transferred to the Burgh School already attended by his younger sister and brother.

The Infant Department, in which I found myself much against my wishes, appeared in 1890, initially to house more advanced courses for senior pupils, but becoming the infants' domain about the turn of the century.

There were four classrooms in the Infant Department of Kirkwall Grammar School. They were divided from each other by sliding wooden partitions, the top section of which was made of panes of clear glass. This method of dividing rooms was most convenient for, when it was desired to assemble the entire Infant School, the partitions were simply pushed back with many a crash and a bang. This happened on Mothers' Day when our mothers took our places in the tiered desks and we entertained them with a much-rehearsed concert.

For most of us the performance consisted of singing in unison. Crosses were chalked on the floor by the teacher and each child marched in and took his place on his allotted cross. The only other Brethren child in the department was not permitted to take part in this innocuous performance. My parents considered such a stance ridiculous and I stood on my cross with the others.

It was a different story when the teacher told us we were going to be taken one afternoon to the local cinema to see 'Snow-white and the Seven Dwarfs'.

'You can't go there,' exclaimed my grandmother in horror. 'Why, it's the devil's house.'

Very, very disappointed, but resigned to the fact, I returned to school. Fear seized me on behalf of my little friend Winnie, my fellow Brownie, for she was going to this place of evil. I warned her of the risk she was taking, using my grandmother's description of the cinema.

'Oooo, I'm tellin' – you swore!' was the indignant rejoinder.

For the rest of the week I lived in a state of fear and trembling because, had she reported me, my name would be in the headmistress's black book and would be read out along with all the other transgressors before the entire department on Friday afternoon. Oh, the shame of it! My relief was immense when name by name was called out and mine was not among them.

The devil's house continued to tempt me throughout my childhood with its colourful posters announcing forthcoming films. I did so want to see the Dionne Quintuplets, but most of all I yearned to see the curly-haired Shirley Temple. A large, shiny, hard-backed *Shirley Temple's Annual* appeared in the paper shop. It was all I wanted for Christmas. I pleaded and pleaded, and my mother granted my heart's desire. From cover to cover I read and re-read it, especially the bits about the child star's very own little house. My mother was aware of all the wishing going on and that summer she had a small wooden hut with one window erected in the garden. My sister and I had a little house of our own.

Sometimes when I see what appears on the small devil's house that takes pride of place in most living rooms these days, I think my grandmother was not far off the beam. The other evening, the smiling announcer uttered in pleasant, happy tones – 'And for you this evening we have a film of crime, violence and corruption'. My grandmother would have likely exclaimed, 'Weel, I don't ken whit the world's comin' tae.' I comfort myself with a flip through the history books. Lately, I've found escape in the legends of the *Orkneyinga Saga*. Reading the stories therein leads me to believe that the ways of the world haven't basically changed all that much. There is certainly plenty of 'crime, violence and corruption' in the pages of this account of Orkney's history.

twelve

I think it is in Genesis we find the phrase 'It is not good for man to live alone'. I think I knew the truth of this even before I could read for I took to walking from leg to leg of the dining-room table murmuring an incantation at each leg – 'I wish I had a doll that could walk and talk.'

One winter's night, when warships in the bay were shooting shafts of light up into the dark sky from their powerful searchlights, and I felt trembly inside as I did when the Aurora Borealis or Northern Lights, commonly called 'the Merry Dancers', flitted and whispered overhead, my mother took me to visit the family next door. Strange, our friendly neighbour was not downstairs with the rest of her family. The father led us upstairs and there seated in bed was the children's mother, holding a baby. It turned out to be a little boy who, when a toddler, had the most charming way of bidding his playmates goodnight – 'Cheerio, see you the morn's day,' he'd say with a cherubic smile.

Spring came and one morning I was sent into a state of overwhelming distress. Mammy wasn't able to get up. Never before had this happened and all the Victorian tales of dying mothers flooded my mind. How could I go to school in those circumstances? It was out of the question. My mother, gently persuasive at first, at last resorted to bribery. If I went to school, instead of the rare and wonderful ha'penny to spend at the Rocky Shop, May would give me a whole penny to buy anything I liked. Such a thing was unheard of! I accepted and went.

I don't remember anything about lunchtime, but when I returned home at 3 o'clock and May told me to go upstairs to my parents' room and see what was there, I lost no time in climbing the stairs.

In the bedroom an old lady called Maudie, dressed in a large white apron and sitting on a chair, was holding a bundle of shawl. My mother, still in bed, told me to go forward to Maudie. I left my post at the door where I had been standing transfixed by the unexpected scene and went over to peer into Maudie's bundle. It contained a baby. 'Is it yours, Maudie?' I enquired.

'No, it's yours,' she smiled. My sister, Lilian had made her debut.

The little girl from next door was waiting for me to go out and play when I came downstairs.

'We've got one too,' I said to her quite nonchalantly and off we went. For hours we used to play ball games against her father's wooden garage door. There were stringent rules. If you made a mistake or let the ball drop in any part of the long ritual your shot was over and when you got your next turn you had to go back to the beginning of the section and start it again. When I played by myself the penalty was even tougher. If I made a mistake I had to go back to the very beginning of the whole ritual.

We started quite simply. Section one was throwing and catching with a different manoeuvre to be performed between each throw and catch. The manoeuvres were named thus – Plainy, Clappy, Rolly, To Backy, Right Hand, Left Hand, High Sketouche, Low Sketouche, Under the Sun, Under the Moon, Toey, Heely, Groundy and Twirl-around. Most of the names are self-explanatory. In High Sketouche you clasped your hands and bent your arms upwards to catch the ball. In Low Sketouche your clasped hands were held downwards and flat to await the ball. Under the Sun and Moon consisted of tossing the ball up from under each leg.

The second section used the same actions as in section one, but each one was performed three times with different ways of throwing the ball. First you threw and caught, second, you threw the ball and let it bounce before catching, and lastly you bounced the ball on the ground before it struck the wall and returned.

The third section consisted of more complicated manoeuvres using your whole body. You stood side on to the wall and bounced the ball towards it from in front of you. Then, still standing side on, you set if off to the wall with a bounce from behind you. Then it was, still from a sideways position, bounced under each leg in turn and this was followed by standing astride facing the wall and bouncing the ball through your legs, and turning round back to the wall you again bounced it through between your legs. Those performances were gone through straightforwardly and then with the addition of 'Clappy' throughout, 'Rolly' throughout and so on till you'd to twirl around each time before catching. If we succeeded in performing all sections faultlessly we sometimes added two-ball play.

My mother passed on two rhymes to say while you kept the ball bouncing up and down on the ground by striking it with the palm of your hand. They were:

Queen, Queen Caroline
Dip your hair in turpentine
Turpentine will make it shine
Queen, Queen Caroline.

Was Caroline George IV's queen whose personal hygiene left much to be desired? The other was:

Mrs Moar by the shore
She has children three or four
The oldest one is twenty four
And married to a sailor.

In My Small Corner

When the sailors come ashore
They do rattle they do roar
When they see Mrs Moar
Walking by the sea-shore.

Our skipping rope games were also played to a pattern. 'What's your husband going to be?' we'd ask, and the player would skip while we chanted – 'A tinker, a tailor, a soldier, a sailor, rich man, poor man, beggar man, thief.' Now what are you going to wear at your wedding? 'Silk, satin, muslin, rags.' You were destined to wear whichever one you tripped on. 'Your house will be – A mansion, a palace, a big hoose, a peedie hoose, a pigsty, a barn.' We skipped to find out how many children there would be – first boys then girls – and so your future was foretold by the skipping rope, your fate each time determined by the word spoken as you tripped. Marriage was the accepted future – no women libbers amongst us.

To play Hopscotch we drew out three squares or rectangles, one above each other, then two side by side followed by a central one above those two, and finishing with another two side by side. Each of the eight square or rectangular shapes – depending on the size and position of the paving stones – was numbered. A flat pebble called a 'peever' was needed. First you hopped up along the shapes, putting both feet down on the two side by side, turned at the top and returned hopping to base. Then you threw your peever on shape one, hopped over it on your progress to the top of the mapped out area, and en route back, had to stop on number two, and standing on one leg, pick up your peever before making your final hop on shape one and home. Next the peever had to be thrown to lie on shape two, and so on till every number had been aimed at. Should the peever land on the wrong number or on a line, that was your shot over until the other players all failed, when it was your turn again.

Those games had their seasons. I couldn't say what they were for they were never defined or spoken about. There just came times when everybody played balls, when skipping ropes appeared, when Hopscotch areas were chalked on every pavement, or when marbles bashed against one another. I carried my beautifully coloured glass marbles in a lovely, dark-green velvet bag with a cord drawstring round the neck to pull it closed.

Clear-cut, definite winter activities, of course, depended on the weather. Snow found us all making slides which we scoured out with our winter boots. These slippery ice paths were very dangerous for unwary adults. Given the right conditions, the sledges were hauled out of the sheds, and on crisp, frosty nights with the cold stars a-twinkle around a pale pearl of moon, we hurtled down the lane, now named Mount Drive, off Cromwell's Road. We never felt the chill, night air, but kept as warm as toast, not only because we were cocooned in clothes, but also by the exertion required to slowly drag the heavy wooden sledges back up to the top of the slope after each speedy ride to the bottom.

Summer had its own highlights. I think it was every other year that our neighbours, the sturdy Shetlanders, invaded our islands with football and hockey sticks. The Orkney *v* Shetland football match took place in the afternoon in the huge, wind-swept Bignold Park. I can't recall the clothes of the footballers, but from the dusky evenings I can picture the Shetland girls in their thick, pink stockings and boots, distinct from the Orcadians, who always gave the impression of being so much more slender in their white blouses, thin black hose and plimsoles. We crowded round the pitches and cheered on our teams till we were hoarse.

The Bignold Park was also the venue for the County Show. The islands and country districts had all held their local shows previously. Now the winning horses, cattle and sheep – I don't remember pigs – were taken to the capital to compete for the championships against the winners throughout the county of Orkney.

Not being knowledgeable about livestock my family did not attend the judging of animals in the morning, but we all hastened up to 'the park' to see the sports and races in the afternoon. How splendid riders looked, wheeling about on their steeds as they waited to be called upon to race. Young men slipped off their long trousers to line up dressed in football shorts and speed round the track.

One year the Rifle Club, of which my cousin Thora was a member, decided to hold a May Day festival on which a May queen would be crowned. Young relatives of the Rifle Club's members were chosen to take part as the queen's attendants and courtiers – I think dressed to represent various countries of the British Empire. One girl I remember adorned helmet, trident and shield as Britannia. When I was eight, I was invited to be a train-bearer with another child of similar size, called Annie. We were both also alike in having short, straight golden hair. Long, white dresses with short puffed sleeves were made by a local dressmaker, whose tedious measurings, proddings and prickings with pins I was relieved to be done with.

The sunny May morning dawned, but my grandmother's passion for curls saw my day marred by the removal of twisting, tugging lengths of rags with which she'd screwed up my hair the previous night. The result – a frizzy mess – was greeted with silent dismay by the lady in charge of costume who encircled our heads with strands of silver ribbon as a finishing touch.

My hair was all forgotten as Annie and I, train-bearers to the newly crowned Queen Violet, drove with her and her ladies-in-waiting through the town in an open horse-drawn carriage. Queen Violet's coronation had taken place in a clearing in a tree plantation round a large establishment called 'Berstane House' just outside the town. Just before the actual ceremony, Annie and I were taken with the Queen to the large drawing-room to be tutored by the wife of the local Sheriff – whose home it was – as to how to bear and arrange the heavy, ermine-trimmed, purple velvet train. Our lesson over, our kindly hostess then rewarded us unwisely with huge unwieldy 'gob-stopping' cubes of butterscotch – what a job it was not to dribble on our pristine white gowns!

High summer days saw the children from our road going to the stony beach to paddle in the sea or catch small fish called 'brandies' in Weyland Burn. Though we carried some of our captive fish home with us soon to expire in our 'cheely chugs', as we called jam jars, I liked it best when we released them back into the burn. Indeed, when I felt the slippery body writhe in my hands it was only to keep face in my society that I didn't immediately set it free. The days were so sunny and warm, the amber water so gentle and cool, the scents of flowers and grasses mingling with the salty tang of the sun-spangled sea so wonderfully pleasant, it seemed a terrible shame to be causing even momentary discomfort and panic in the breast of a small fish.

Near Weyland Burn two white-topped stone walls guarded Cromwell's Road from the sea. They were known simply as 'the first white dyke' and 'the second white dyke'. At one spot, water gurgled out of the second white dyke. This was called 'The Lady's Well' and on hot days we sipped its cool water out of shells.

It was one such summer scene that I wrote about when Robert Rendall set an essay for our Sunday School Class. The title was either 'My idea of Heaven' or 'What I think Heaven will be like'. Some more serious minded scholars looked up Revelation and based their accounts on St John's visions, but I won the prize. Maybe not surprising since Robert, who was the judge of our efforts, took great delight in the countryside and in the moods of the elements. As he stated in his poem 'Birsay', which I've already quoted, he hated being shackled in the town to a trade. He made his escape as often as he could, at one point even buying a croft house at Scapa with an acre or two of land on which he could live as a true countryman.

One of the nicest parties I was ever at was in his Scapa cottage. Robert always had unusual ideas, and part of our entertainment was having our silhouettes drawn and cut out. The silhouettes were made by throwing the shadows of our profiles on paper by the light of an oil lamp. There was no electricity or running water.

We must have walked the three or so miles out to Robert's cottage, but anyhow it would have been a straightforward walk and not like the journey I made to one party in town. Another guest and I let it be known at school that we didn't know how to get to our hostess's house. 'I'll take you,' volunteered my hair-pulling tormentor of the Baby Class. We climbed walls, we ran through peoples' cabbage patches, we trampled through well-kept herbeceous borders – all in the wake of our leader who insisted this was the only way to reach the party. We did eventually get there but what a sight we must have looked!. It was no surprise to me to see in a newspaper many years later, a picture of this young woman, now a sergeant in the ATS supervising recruits on a rifle range. I can imagine that it would have suited her fine to head the charge across a battlefield.

Autumn, too, welcomed a range of activities unique to my small corner. That was the season of 'the market'. My grandmother always spoke of 'the Lammas market' and looked forward to getting her 'fairing' which I used to happily choose for her. The market of my childhood, as I often heard May sigh, was not the same as it used to be. In her day it had been an exciting, quite marvellous affair, and cousins from North Ronaldsay and the island of Sanday had flocked to town to enjoy it, merrily bedding down on the floor – for my family's flats were already filled to capacity – but that only added to the fun.

Even so, I thrilled as I approached the crowded area known as 'The Crafty', and heard the blaring music that filled the air. When you got nearer there were booths painted in garish colours, lit up with coloured lights and crammed with glorious prizes to be won.

In vain did I throw wooden balls at the coconut shy. So great was my desire for this strange, shaggy brown object that my father offered to buy one from the woman in charge. No, she wouldn't sell. You had to play the game. Eventually, my father won a coconut for me, and I still remember the feeling of sinking my teeth into the white chewy flesh and how I even enjoyed its rather bland milk.

My father, an ex-machine gunner who, once having scored several bulls' eyes on an army rifle range, intentionally shot off target thereafter to avoid being chosen for a sniper, always had a go with the rifles at the shooting stalls. But alas, never did he win one of the beautiful big teddies or canteens of cutlery or china tea-sets. Perhaps an ashtray, a key-ring or bottle opener was handed over, maybe some small doll for me, but we didn't care; it was all a gamble, but a gay, carefree one. Far more important to find a partner for the swing boat. In we both jumped, grabbing and pulling the two ropes at either end which hoisted the heavy swing higher and higher. Up and up we swung, nearly bouncing off the wooden seats as we soared – and all the time shrieking with delight as our stomachs did somersaults!

Besides the booths and amusements, the tents of the fortune-telling gypsies and huge constructions containing distorting mirrors or that the death-defying motorcycle show called 'The Wall of Death', all brought from 'the sooth' – the mainland of Scotland – local traders, too, set up stalls. I remember one selling ice-cream and mouth-watering slices of juicy, golden melon. The local chip van did a roaring trade, whetting the appetite with its tantalising cooking smells, and, oh, how splendid did the fat, golden-brown, piping-hot chips taste out of their greasy paper pokes that toasted your cold hands. The nights were drawing in – summer over, winter coming – and this bustling, noisy area filled with light, colour and music became more exciting as twilight turned to night. It brought an interlude of joy and pleasure touched with a sense of strangeness and excitement between the long, light days and short dusky nights of summer, and the short days and long, dark nights of winter.

thirteen

One morning our art class in the Secondary Department of Kirkwall Grammar School was interrupted by the arrival of a new girl. She was very attractive, with olive skin, large grey eyes fringed with long, dark lashes. Her chestnut hair lay in soft waves over her head and hung in a thick plait down her back. Unlike our gym dresses, with their bulky box pleats, her navy tunic was in a simple, uncluttered pinafore style with a low square neck and neat bodice that fitted in at the waist and from which the plain skirt flared slightly. She had a mellow, contralto voice and spoke with an English accent. She was an evacuee.

I think she came from Liverpool. She'd been evacuated to stay with Orcadian relatives as our group of islands, looking so nationally unimportant in their box set in the top corner of the map, were seen as likely to be ignored by the enemy. She arrived just in time to hear the 'drum-drum-drum' of the German Junkers above Orkney and the sirens wail their dismal moans filled with foreboding. When this heart-chilling howling rose and fell, persistent and all-intruding, and we were in school, those of us within ten minutes' running distance of home sped off, taking every short-cut we knew. As we flew along, sometimes the drone of the enemy's engines pounded in our ears; sometimes the crack of gunfire sent us scurrying for shelter in the nearest house. The windows, bandaged with criss-crossing strips of gummed paper, rattled with each blast, and you felt as though every bone and nerve in your body shuddered with them, as you fearfully cowered in dark cupboards under the stairs. The once peaceful nights safe in your own bed were a thing of the past. We all assembled in the blacked-out living-room at the back of the house, torn from sleep by the woebegone, warning notes, holding our breath as a Junker whined downwards, diving to pepper the beach with bullets, thinking he was attacking the aerodrome by the opposite shore.

We really had no reason to feel surprised that the German Air Force paid us so much unwelcome attention at the beginning of the Second World War. Ships of the Royal Navy lay in Scapa Flow, and there were Fleet Air Arm, Air Force and Army bases scattered over the Mainland.

Soon Kirkwallians were fitted with gas masks and told to arrange for emergency homes in the country districts in case they had to be evacuated. Brethren acquaintances in Shapinsay volunteered to take my family. They were 'undiluted' Brethren and would have neither a radio nor a newspaper in their house. There would be no *Bulletin* for the not-to-be-missed cartoon featuring Scottikin, a perky Scottie dog, and no *Daily Express* in which to follow unfailingly the adventures of Rupert Bear. Fortunately, cheery, roly-poly Mary Ann, her husband, Francis and her father, dear, bearded 'Uncle' Willie, relatives in the parish of Tankerness, offered shelter, too, and my family decided that theirs was the home we would go to, should the need arise.

As it happened, we did not have to be evacuated, but a stay in the Old Schoolhouse, Tankerness, would have been no hardship, for we had spent many happy holidays there. The very fact that the long, low house had been a school made it an interesting place straightaway. There was a feeling of excitement about living where children of long ago had pored over books and practised their copperplate with ink-stained fingers. It was as if there was only a fragile veil between present and past, and if you concentrated hard enough you could tear that veil of time and see the rooms set out and peopled as they once had been.

Next to the house stood a small church. Never before having been close to a place of worship which was totally deserted, this was a new experience. There was something liberating about being able to run round the building and throw balls against its walls and over its roof. What luck it seemed to have a little church to yourself – a little church you were free to treat in a familiar fashion. It seemed rather daring to do so. But, oh, the panic in our breasts that fateful day when one of a group of girls, who'd come to play, threw the ball too low and broke two of the square, pinky panes in a window.

'Never mind,' said Mary Ann when we confessed to her, 'say nothing about it. I know somebody who'll mend it, and can be depended upon to keep his mouth shut.' And so it was done. From then on one window in that little church had two squares of plain glass among its pink panes. I wonder if anybody, having a look round when bored with the sermon, spotted them and pondered.

My parents certainly were not bored with one sermon they heard there. They both came back to Old Schoolhouse smiling broadly and in a very happy frame of mind. The minister's words had been of a cheering nature we gathered, but the only bit of his sermon I recall them passing on to us was the closing sentence which left me feeling slightly baffled. 'Don't say good-bye – just Cheerio,' the minister had advised the congregation. Strange thing for a minister to say thought I. After all, 'good-bye' was short for 'God be with you'. But my parents seemed so delighted that I'm glad to say I had enough sense to keep my thoughts to myself on that occasion.

The old gentleman who was minister was surely blessed with a happy, humorous disposition. I remember another of his sayings. This one was uttered to my father when they both were travelling on a train from Inverness to Thurso. The train stopped at every single small station along the line and so took a very long time to reach its destination. 'Can you tell me,' the minister asked my father, 'where we hear of this train in the Bible?'

'I'm afraid I can't,' replied my father after some thought.

'"He made the creeping thing also."'

Memories of an Orkney Childhood

The group of girls who came to play invited us back to their homes. They lived on nearby farms and so we had fields to race over, building up tremendous appetites for the banquets spread lavishly on the tables in the farmhouse kitchens.

Two other girls from Kirkwall came to stay in an empty manse about a couple of miles from Schoolhouse. With permits required to get in and out of Orkney, people restricted their holidays to the country parishes and islands. We were invited to the spacious manse to play in its large garden. My sister and I strolled along the roads those beautiful, sunny mornings, sandal-shod and dressed in cotton summer dresses. We never failed to stop and lean on the dyke by the meal mill and watch the giant wheel rotate under the power of the splashing water that slurped and slithered over its paddle blades. There was another interesting water feature in the manse itself. In the large, airy hall stood a metal pump and we used to take it in turns to pump the heavy metal handle up and down and up and down just so we could watch the crystal clear water gush out of the nozzle.

Much further along the road to the manse was the 'big house' of the neighbourhood – the Hall of Tankerness. Mary Ann and her son, Stewart, used to accompany us to the beach below the Hall, where we paddled, played and picnicked, not, in my case, feeling entirely carefree, for our journey had included crossing a field where a big black bull was master, and our return meant hurrying past him again with wildly beating heart and jellied legs that would not move fast enough.

I wish somebody at the time had told me something of the past of the place. In the twelfth century, a Norse chieftain, Erling by name, lived on the site of the Hall of Tankerness. One Friday morning as the sun rose, Erling saw five ships belonging to Earl Paul off-shore. Then twelve enemy longships came round the Moul Head of Deerness. Erling and his sons watched as Earl Paul had his ships fastened together and then made their way to the Earl's ship. There they saw in the forecastle one of Earl Paul's right-hand men – the huge, ugly Sweyn Breastrope who spent his summers on raids of plunder and slaughter, and his winters by the side of the Earl. When the quiet darkness descended he was often to be seen slipping out of the great hall to go and sit in the open, and, under the dark cloak of night, by muttering incantations, call up the dead to ask their advice and glean knowledge of the future.

Erling and his sons wanted to join the Earl's side, but the warships were already manned to capacity. However, Earl Paul accepted their offer of help and set them to loading him up with ammunition. This took the form of stones, broken, if need be, to a suitable size, to be employed as missiles.

It was one of Erling's boulders that saved the day. Olvir Rosta, ally of the threatening Rognvald, and also a claimant for a share of Paul's earldom, drove the powerful Sweyn Breastrope and his supporters from the forecastle and boarded the Earl's ship. Earl Paul leapt from the quarter deck to close with Olvir, who, seeing the Earl advancing, hurled a spear at him. The Earl using his shield warded off the weapon successfully, but tumbled down on the deck. The sight of the earl lying prostrate caused a great uproar, and much shouting, but if the opposition's shouting was of triumph it was short-lived for Sweyn Breastrope immediately grasped a huge chunk of stone, took aim and threw. It struck Olvir a mighty blow on the chest which toppled him overboard, and he disappeared under the water. Some of his men managed to get hold of him and haul him on to his own ship, but though on regaining consciousness, he urged his men to fight on, they continued to cut their ships loose and take flight leaving five ships behind for Earl Paul to commandeer and fit out to fight another day.

Concerned more with making a living rather than extinguishing it, the herring boats of the nineteenth and early twentieth centuries were common sights in the sea below the Hall of Tankerness. Along the shore assembled their back-up people – the women who gutted and packed the fish, the coopers who dealt with the barrels.

From 1630–1951 the Hall itself was the country house of the Baikie family. In 1683 William Baikie founded the Kirkwall Library and so it seems appropriate that the present museum in Kirkwall is lodged in the Baikies' sixteenth-century town house, Tankerness House.

We had taken our bicycles out to Old Schoolhouse for our holidays and they came in quite useful for longer jaunts. Down a soft grassy path by a limpid amber burn bordered by sweet-scented, wild pink roses we wheeled our bykes and, on reaching the main road headed east towards our goal: the parish of Deerness. A peninsula, its link with the mainland being an isthmus only 50–100 yards wide, it holds the fairy mound of Dingishowe. Deerness was the 'animal ness' of the Norsemen who thought the Moul of Deerness, the peninsula's tapered north-eastern point, resembled the snout of an animal.

Soon we were gazing across the sea at the small island of Copinsay which had been owned by a Norseman called Kolbein, who named it *Kolbeinsay* after himself and meaning 'isle of Kolbein'. The white lighthouse station perched on the topmost edge of the island dominated the scene, but a dark-coloured building could be discerned down near the low landward shore. There cousins of ours had lived – a family of fourteen. Because of the dangerous cliffs that surrounded them, the children of a family who had lived there before our cousins were put on tethers for safety. Because of those same steep cliffs Copinsay has been made into a bird sanctuary in memory of James Fisher, the ornithologist.

We visited an elderly relative of my mother who lived in Deerness. This old lady's main concern that day was that a man she'd commissioned to come and shoot pigeons had failed to appear. The birds had prospered and multiplied in her small courtyard mainly, she suspected, because they gorged themselves on the food she put out for her hens. How I hoped the man with the gun delayed his coming till we had departed.

Many, many years after my family's cycling foray into Deerness, I read some of its history and re-visited some of its places of interest. Not quite at the tip of the snout of Deerness is another small island, the Brough of Deerness. During the sixteenth century, and nobody knows for how long before, pilgrims made their barefooted way on hands and knees up the dangerous path that stretches from the beach and along the very edge of the precipitous side of the Brough right to the cliff top. On the grassy top was a chapel, cells for monks and a well of fresh, spring water. The ritual of the pilgrimage consisted of walking round the church two or three times, hands clasped and knees bent, every now and again throwing water and stones behind.

This chapel has since been excavated and put in an orderly condition.

Other excavations in Deerness have found layers of dwellings at the house of Skaill. Not surprising some of those dwellings date from the Norse era for the house's name, 'Skaill', is from the Norse, *skali*, meaning 'the hall'. It is thought that in its vicinity stood the eleventh-century hall of Amundi and his son, Thorkel. The hard, unpopular Earl Einar was ruling part of Orkney at that time. The ordinary people felt oppressed by his demands on them and begged Amundi to become their spokesman. Amundi was a well off person who wielded considerable power in the land, but he declined to play the part of mediator.

The people then approached his son Thorkel, who pleaded successfully with Einar at first, but only succeeded in riling the Earl and making matters worse at their second meeting. The furious Earl brought their meeting to an abrupt close, muttering that either he or Thorkel would not depart from the 'thing' unharmed.

Amundi, who had disapproved of his son's taking on the role of mediator, told Thorkel to leave Orkney so that Einar could do him no injury. Thorkel, who won a reputation for wisdom and good sense, spent his time of self-imposed exile 'making friends and influencing people'. He became foster-father to the young Earl Thorfinn, brother of Einar and Brusi who were ruling the earldom between them at that time. On Thorfinn's advice Thorkel visited King Olaf in Norway, and they became great friends.

When Thorkel eventually did accompany Thorfinn to Orkney to support the young Earl of Caithness and Sutherland which was Thorfinn's title, in his bid for what he considered was his rightful share of the earldom of Orkney, Earl Brusi tried to pour oil on troubled waters. One of his plans for reconciliation contained an arrangement whereby Einar and Thorkel were to agree to be friends and give banquets for each other.

Thorkel's feast was the first to take place, and was of course held in his hall in Deerness. Einar attended with his bodyguard, but did not enjoy himself to judge from his gloomy countenance. It turned out he was right to feel uneasy. As he waited for Thorkel, who was to go along with him when he left, there were many comings and goings and much delay. Earl Einar waiting impatiently by the fire at length enquired if

Thorkel was now ready. Thorkel replied that he was, and struck the earl such a blow on the head that he fell into the fire.

Hallvard an Icelandic crony of Thorkel's remarked to the amazed company – 'I never saw people with so little presence of mind as you who are here. Why do you not take the Earl out of the fire?' He then whacked Einar's skull with his axe, and he and Thorkel made themselves scarce and joined Thorkel's armed men who were waiting outside. Such was Thorkel's high reputation that Einar's friends could not believe their senses. They stood dumbfounded.

Thorkel was soon on his way to his friend King Olaf who made no secret of his delight at being rid of Einar who had offended him in the past.

It was much later in life that I visited the huge gash in the earth, a blowhole called the 'Gloup of Deerness' and the memorial tower beside the western shore, which had been built to keep in mind the tragic end of Covenanters who were drowned near this place. They had been taken prisoner at the Battle of Bothwell Bridge in 1679 and were being transported as slaves to the American colonies. Most of them were battened down beneath hatches, and so had no chance at all of escape when a fierce gale battered the ship to pieces.

When our Tankerness holidays ended, it wasn't a final goodbye; a five-mile cycle ride renewed our acquaintance with Old Schoolhouse, where we sometimes collected rakes and pails and made our way down to the sands below the house to collect cockles. We so enjoyed raking the sands and gathering up the cockles as a setting sun spilled glorious colour on the calm water, the sea-birds crying overhead and the smells of salty sea and seaweed mingling with that of tarred boats and their ropes. One friend, however, delighted more in the cockle gathering than in the actual eating of them. When she sat down to her supper afterwards and found she didn't like them – 'They are so squelchy,' she complained – the look on her face told of the enormous disappointment she felt.

One summer's evening I took a cousin from Canada to Old Schoolhouse. He had been sent over to Britain with the Canadian Air Force and came to Orkney for his leaves. 'Uncle' Willie of the huge bushy beard sat by the fire smoking his pipe as usual, but when my cousin, Johnny, offered him a cigarette he accepted one with alacrity. Johnny applied his cigarette lighter to the tip which was almost all that could be seen among Uncle Willie's luxuriant whiskers. As we cycled home, Johnny, smiling quizzically, drawled, 'I sure thought I was starting a bush fire there.'

A young family friend from the Air Force accompanied me on one cycle run to Tankerness. It was a beautiful summer evening and Gordon and I were going to attend a concert performed by the young people of the parish in the local school. A cowboy sang 'The Red River Valley' and other songs from America's west. A line of chorus girls in frilly skirts and with small, flower-like crowns perched on their heads, danced and sang 'Chocolate Soldier from the USA' among other war-time ditties. Outside influences were making themselves felt in the islands.

I had met Gordon through the Salvation Army. All the locals adopted the service people who attended the meetings, and entertained them in their houses. Those young men also swelled our numbers in the newly started Salvation Army Youth Group called 'The Torchbearers'. Their lively presence added greatly to our enjoyment of table tennis tournaments and other games, and I remember the fun and laughter which echoed as we worked at various handicrafts By and by it was decided that The Torchbearers perform a play and the title we arrived at was 'Youth at the Crossroads'. 'Youth', represented by me, stood hesitatingly at a crossroads in life and there was visited by representatives of various routes that could be followed. 'Education' in cap and gown had to be rejected, as did 'Pleasure' in evening dress and jewels. Of course, 'Christianity', clothed in white with a blue cloak, won the day, and was followed by 'Service', in Salvationist's uniform, which was also accepted.

In the finale, 'youth' was supposed to appear in Salvation Army uniform, but this youth had a stalwart Brethren father determined that the Salvation Army would not 'get' his daughter. At long last, after much heated discussion, he agreed to my wearing the bonnet just as long as I promised to remove it the minute the play was over. Never mind, I'd had my first part in a play – on stage, acting a part at last, though I must say the accompanying nervousness was not comfortable.

The Brethren meetings, too, had zipped up a little with the injection of service personnel. A local doctor took over the evening Gospel meeting when the hall was packed with men of the forces. His musical abilities were up to organising the singing and his powerful personality, his certainty that what he believed was absolutely right, enabled him to preach with conviction. I for one hung on his every word and was sure there was no question for which he wouldn't have an answer. Once, our Religious Education teacher unwisely threw open the class for a day of religious questions of any kind. One boy, the son of an atheist, asked – 'If Eve was the only woman and she had three sons, where did the rest of the population come from?' The teacher was flummoxed and so was I. My beliefs had received a body blow for I'd been brought up to believe that every word in the Bible was absolutely true as it stood in the James VI version. I hastened to the Doctor. He'd have an answer, I felt sure. He did. 'It says,' he explained, 'that Adam and Eve had many sons and daughters, and things were so arranged then that the daughters had children to their brothers.'

Strange as it may sound, I was perfectly satisfied with his answer.

The doctor and his wife were as thoughtful to the material needs of the service men as they were to the spiritual. After the hymns and the homily, trays of food and pots of tea were provided. They also held a discussion circle in their home on Saturday evenings, where – it not being held in the actual Brethren hall – women were permitted to take part. We sang hymns, read aloud studies we'd made of Biblical characters and played a rather good Bible game.

'I'm thinking of a man whose name begins with 'A' who killed a sheep.'

'Was he murdered by his brother?'

'No, it wasn't Abel.'

'Did angels visit him?'

'Yes, it was Abraham.'

Young person after young person went to the doctor and expressed the desire to be baptised and become a member of the Brethren. Every time I opened my Bible, there was God telling me to do likewise. But I was terrified of being laid under the water as I'd witnessed happening to

Maggie and Harry all those years ago. I had refused to attend any baptism after that childhood experience. My fear was compounded by the thought of being part of the public spectacle into which the doctor had transformed the services by insisting they be carried out on Sunday afternoons. Previously, they'd been done in the quiet morning with only Brethren spectators. Now people from the town crowded out to the beach below Greenfield to view the ceremony. That, I decided, I could not endure. What if I made a fool of myself going under or coming out of the water?

At last, after months of stress and strain, I went to see the Doctor. He was delighted the Lord had told me to be baptised, but was it fear of man that made me insist it be carried out in the early morning? 'No,' I lied for I knew only too well he'd not let me off with that. I explained I wanted to be baptised and then go straight into the meeting the same morning. Well, I was sure God wanted me to be baptised because my Bible would only open at passages on that subject, but I'd had no call from above to join the Brethren – it just helped along my excuse for not being baptised in front of the population of Kirkwall.

The morning of my baptism was grey and rain pellets pitted the smooth, grey bay outside my window. 'How could God let it rain that special day?' I wondered.

My parents and I, carrying a little case full of clothes, walked the mile or so out Cromwell's Road to the house of Greenfield. In the front parlour, chairs were set out in rows for the preliminary service. I was taken to a bedroom where I removed my clothes and put on a pale-lemon summer dress and gym shoes on my bare feet. I was given an old fawn raincoat to keep me warm. Into its pocket I pushed a red swimming cap. One of the elders of 'the meeting', as the assembly was usually called, instructed me as to how I was to hold his hands, and when I was to take a deep breath and hold it as he lowered me backwards into the water.

I then joined the congregation in the front parlour for the service at which some of the verses on baptism that had been haunting me for so long were read out. Prayers were said and hymns sung, and then we all made our way down the long, winding avenue to the stony beach. I was still perplexed that the day was dull and rainy. After all, here was I about to please God by obeying his command.

Then I removed the raincoat and the elder and I waded out into the sea. He prayed and then immersed me in the water. I rose happy and smiling. The ordeal was over. I hadn't made a fool of myself and at that moment the sun appeared from among the grey clouds and shone on the scene. To my overworked imagination, it was like a sign of approval from on high. My old sinful self had been symbolically laid in the grave with Christ and now a new person had risen – who'd never do a bad action, never speak a wrong word, never think an unworthy thought. So had I planned. This was to be the beginning of a new and saintly era. Alas, it didn't work out like that.

The time came for me to leave home and go south to a Teachers' Training College. The Doctor warned me I'd be told dreadful, untrue things – evolutionary theories and the like. I must shut my ears to them, close my mind to all such heresies and associate only with other true Christians of like mind.

I vividly recall the dreaded day of my departure. As I walked slowly to the gate, I glanced back at the kitchen window to see my mother weeping. I desperately wanted to rush back to her, but my cousin Jean was waiting for me, my place at College and Jean's at University had been accepted and all arrangements had been made for our lodging in Edinburgh. It seemed impossible to back out now. And so, I ventured out into the world – a very feeble, flickering candle moving very unsteadily away from its small corner.

Glossary

bonie words prayers; from the old Norse 'bonie', meaning 'blessed'

buddo or budda a term of endearment; from an Old Norse word meaning 'offspring'

clapshot an Orcadian dish composed of turnips, potatoes and onion cooked and mashed together

creepie a low stool with a hole in the centre of the seat

cuithe second year saithe or coal fish

gey coorsh rather tough to the touch

peedie small

peedie greet a little weep

wir our

Other books you might enjoy:

Blithe and Braw: Nostalgic and Neglected Scots Poems
Anne Forsyth (edited)
ISBN: 1 898218 25 0   £5.99

Canty and Couthie: Familiar and Forgotten Scots Poems
Anne Forsyth (edited)
ISBN: 1 898218 04 8   £5.99

I Was Not Alone: Memoirs of a Boy Soldier in 1935
Robert Dick
ISBN: 1 84017 006 9   £9.99

My Captains: Memoirs of a Fisherman
Tom Ralston
ISBN: 1 898218 27 7   £4.95

North East Song & Story: An Anthology of Song & Verse Traditional to North-East Scotland
W. Morrice Wilson (edited)
ISBN: 1 898218 81 1   £9.99

Roots in a Northern Landscape
Gordon Lawrence (edited)
ISBN: 1 898218 79 X   £7.95

To the Edge: Confessions of a Lifeboat Coxswain
Tom Ralston
ISBN: 1 898218 64 1   £5.95

To order any of the above, or to request a free copy of
our complete catalogue, please contact
Scottish Cultural Press at Unit 13d, Newbattle Abbey Business Annexe,
Newbattle Road, Dalkeith EH22 3LJ Scotland
Tel: +44 (0)131 660 6366 ~ Fax: +44 (0)131 660 6414
Email: info@scottishbooks.com
or visit our website at: **www.scottishbooks.com**